POSTAL REVENGE

BY

CAROLYN ROSE

Bloomington, IN  Milton Keynes, UK

authorHOUSE®

AuthorHouse™
1663 Liberty Drive, Suite 200
Bloomington, IN 47403
www.authorhouse.com
Phone: 1-800-839-8640

AuthorHouse™ UK Ltd.
500 Avebury Boulevard
Central Milton Keynes, MK9 2BE
www.authorhouse.co.uk
Phone: 08001974150

This book is a work of non-fiction. Unless otherwise noted, the author and the publisher make no explicit guarantees as to the accuracy of the information contained in this book and in some cases, names of people and places have been altered to protect their privacy.

First published by AuthorHouse 2/13/2007

ISBN: 978-1-4259-8344-4 (sc)

Library of Congress Control Number: 2006910636

Printed in the United States of America
Bloomington, Indiana

This book is printed on acid-free paper.

DEDICATION

This book is dedicated to the men and women that have served there time in the Postal Service and did a great job.

To those that have been abused by the system whether served as a Postmaster, Clerk, Carrier or a Mail Handler, this goes out to you.

The names and locations have been changed to protect the innocent.

Special thank you goes out to my husband that has been so supportive with my work.

PREFACE

This book shows how the Postal Service performs and manages all the mail that comes in and the people that give all they have to perform the duties required of them to get the mail out as soon as possible.

This book tell's you what happens during Christmas time and how much mail comes into each and every Post Office facility and is process.

This is a true story of one man's postal career that came to the point that he could not take anymore abuse from the foreman and then Steve had a plan of shooting him to death and then turning the gun on himself. His wife was about to leave him and take his children. He felt he had nothing else to live for.

This book gives insight to how the postal service is ran. The many tests that are required to get the position and keep it. The stress that is involved with working for the postal service and the duties of employment.

These are true stories of what has gone on in the walls of the postal service buildings and the people's lives.

I have been asked to give my opinion of a solution to the killing inside the postal service. I have studied this problem and giving details of changing the form of the management system of the employee's. We need to work for a common goal and to take care of our resources and not to abuse them until they cannot take it any longer and everyone loses.

We need the military form out of the United States Postal Service job performance duties.

The names and places have been changed to protect the privacy of those that were involved.

CONTENTS

CHAPTER ONE
GETTING THE JOB

I was just out of high school and was making only the local wage and my husband who was ten years older then I was, was making the same per hour. I long to do something that paid a great deal more money. I knew that we would never get a better life if I did not look for something that paid better.

You see, my husband was a very laided back and enjoyed his model airplanes and a general job was just fine with him, even though he was labeled a genius by his score, he could not find a job that paid better per his intelligence. So, I decided that I would look for a better job. I was working at a J C Penney's catalog store and was working the counter as a customer service clerk and helped people with their orders.

One day a postal carrier lady came up to my counter and after helping her with order that she placed, I asked her, how did you get your job at the Postal Service? She said, that she went down to the main Post Office which is located in the down town area. Then you go up to the second floor where you will see the Personnel Office and go in and tell them that you would like to apply for a postal position. Be sure to ask what job titles are available to apply for. She then said, it is a very long application so be ready to spend at least an hour to fill this application out. They will do a background check on you and a personal report of your past employment. This is a federal job, you know.

Then once that is done, they will send out a letter telling you to come in a certain date and time to complete the post office test. Then they will send out a letter stating your score of that test. Then you will be placed on the roster, which is the list of people that have pasted the test per grade and who they can call upon to come in to start the hiring process.

She then told me that there are ten differed job areas that you can apply for.

1) Occupations: Another word for office personnel.
2) Distribution Clerk/Machine and Flat Sorting Operators field: which covers a great multitude area in the Post Office.
3) Mail Handler/Processor: which will work at airport facilities and all post offices.
4) Custodian & Custodial Laborer field
5) Data Conversion Operators
6) Maintenance Positions
7) Motor Vehicle Operator
8) City Carrier & Clerk
9) Automated Mark Up Clerk
10) Processing, Distribution & Delivery: OCR machines.

The optical carrier machines are the machines that you see on TV that makes the mail go through so fast and the mail goes to a particular tray of that zip code and then is boxed up to go to that destination.

I told her thank you so much. I will look into this. I am very grateful for all of your information.

So, I went down town to the main Postal Service building and went up to that floor and asked about what positions they had available to apply for. She told me that the only position available was the Clerk position. I then asked for an application. She said, please bring it back and then we will let you know when the test will be. We will mail you a notice to come take the test and where it will be located act, which building of the postal service. Don't worry, there will also be a practices test enclosed with your letter so that you can study before the test. It is an easy test.

I did a little homework on my own after I got the application from that lady. I learned that the Postal Service employs 252,285 workers – more than any other Fortune 500 company. And they generate more then 60 billion dollars in sales annually.

The Postal Service had said that over half of all workers are mail carriers and clerks and the remaining 200,000 + workers are employed in hundreds of occupations from janitors and truck drivers to accountants, personnel specialists, electronics technicians and engineers. They told me that the process would be like this: Examinations, I would take many examinations that would measure or evaluate my knowledge skills and abilities to predict probable future work performance.

Passing examination scores would be from 70 to 100 percent. Then by passing I would be on the register list. This list contains applicant names and other information including an examination rating and or results of an evaluation process. My name would be placed on the register in numerical score order. Then after that, I would be tested for my suitability. This evaluation includes a review of my: 1) Applicants work history, 2) Criminal conviction history, 3) Personal interview skill, 4) Medical assessment. I found out that medical assessment is an example of suitability screening that occurs after the job offer. The Rehabilitation Act of 1973 prohibits the Postal Service from inquiring into an applicant's medical suitability until a bona fide job offer is made. Medical assessment is done after selecting an applicant who has met all other suitability requirements. After an applicant is hired, a career employee's job performance is evaluated during the probationary period. Fingerprints are submitted for a special agency check to be performed by the Office of Personnel Management to ensure that there is no derogatory information about the individual that has not been discovered in the screening process.

One of the post offices ways of thinking is, "Good things come to those who wait, as long as you work like hell while you wait."

My job would be a Distribution Clerk, the job description is as follows: To separate mail in a post office, terminal, airport mail facility or other postal facility in accordance with established schemes, including incoming or outgoing mail or other. I was about to learn many schemes. You must pass this test in three months. You can pass with a score of 75 percent.

After applying with the Postal Service, I waited for a letter to come in the mail that would say, come in on this date and take the test and I would do my best to pass it and then be earning an excellent income and have a great life. I wanted to better myself.

Each week I would wonder if my husband and I would get a letter in the mail from the U.S. Postal Service saying; please come to this location at this time and to be prepared to take the postal service exam for being hired. My husband went with me to the downtown Post Office and applied with me that day. He put in for a mail handler position.

No word or letter had come. We soon just got back to our lives and worked and did our crafts on the weekends. It wasn't until two years later that I received a letter in the mail. It was a very hot day. I remember that summer. One of us went to get the mail; there it was a letter to Carolyn. The letter said, please report Monday morning at 9:00 a.m. at the main Post Office to take the Postal exam for the position of Machine Distribution Clerk which will pay $9.61 an hour.

I was so excited; we were in such bad financial shape. My husband was without a job, I was working so hard and I just knew that God was helping us to make it.

I was so nervous that morning. I could not eat breakfast. I arrived at the Post Office about an hour and a half early. I looked around in the cafeteria and had a cup of coffee. Ok, it is time to go into the room. I was so nervous. I had to be able to pass all these tests. But, I have been never good at passing tests. I was a very slow learning student in school when I was younger but I must pass this, we have to survive. I must do it....

The instructor brought all of us into a large room there was about twenty people, all mixed ages and nationalities.

I made sure that I paid attention to every word that was said by the instructor. Ok, here comes the test. The first was an eye test, to check our vision. Next to a room to lift a bag that weighed was seventy pounds that we must lift up to our waist. I did it I was able to lift the seventy pound bag of mail. Then we all went back to the main room.

We then got temporary badges to get in to the building and out again. He then explained about the job that we would be working. It would be a long machine that twelve people would be sitting on at one time and have two people loading the trays of first class mail, letter mail, onto the machine for the people sitting down to key in the zip code. Then there would be two other people in the back of the machine; they would clean out all the slots where the mail would fall. They would run back and fourth behind the machine for fifteen minutes and do nothing but clean all the mail out and put that mail into trays, those trays would go up the convayerbelt that would go to the truck dock for dispatch.

Now came time for the rest of the testing. I sat down and took a deep breath and began, I also prayed to God to help me do this.

The instructor asked me to go first. I had to sit at the beginning of this test machine, just like the one that we saw on the floor. There was to be one hundred cards with zip codes on them that would go by the keyboard and then I would need to see the first three digits of that zip code and type in the first three. I need to not miss anymore then three. Then I would continue to the next testing.

Ok, the first card went by and I typed the first three digits, then the next and the next and took a breath of fresh air through it and remained focused on what I was doing, now it was over, I wondered how did I do... The instructor said that I had only missed...one. I could not believe my ears, I was so happy, now I knew that I could do this. I was sure that I could go on.

It was now lunchtime, we all seemed to be worn out from being nervous. It was nice to sit down and relax. Some of the people that have not taken the test yet seemed to be very nervous still because they were not go at typing. They were going to try very hard to pass the test, they said. Ok, lunch was over. We had to go back to the testing room. Everyone, the first test is over. I wondered how everyone did on it. He said, well you all have passed with flying colors. You all have qualified to be employed by the U.S. Postal Service. Twenty of us from all types of backgrounds and have lived all over the United States and including the Philippines.

Our group was five women and seven men. The tallest and quietest was Tom; he was married and had no children yet. Betsy was about my size and skinny and very meek and quite type. Jim was half country style man and half hippy type. Now then there was Jesse, he was the don-won of lovers as he put it, he had many lovers and did not mind coming on to the woman and trying to get her into bed. Then there was Steve, he was a nice looking, quite and the kind of guy that keep to himself, and he was a married man and had two children. Robin was an older man in his forties, I believe forty-two. Mark was a single, cute and really loved music. Carolyn, that's me, I was a short, always smiling and busty woman that enjoyed working hard. Sue, she was a very overweight woman, she complain about everything and just did not want to work. Marietta was a beautiful Latino woman in her thirties and was a very hard worker that keeps to her. Denise was a very outgoing friendly California lady. I enjoyed her laughter very much. Last then was Ricky, he was my friend and a Christian that did not mind showing it. He was a married man that I knew that I could talk with and he respected me and I respected him but needed each other as a Christian Brother and sister. He always smiled, too.

We all past all of the tests and now we were Letter Sorting Machine clerks. Our crew made up a twelve people crew who worked on one of the machines. We all went through hours of trying to memorize all the zip codes and codes to certain zip codes. We need to type the three digits each second, we will see sixty letters per minute. We all took turns sitting down for a half an hour and did our keying of the zip codes that we saw and then would get up while another person came and took our place on the machine so then we could go around the machine to clean the back side of it. It was only fifteen minutes back there but it went by pretty fast and then back to the front side to sit in the console behind the one we were previously at. Then stay there for a half an hour and do it all over again for the rest of the night. Our breaks and lunchtime is the only time we had to ourselves. We were able to relax for fifteen minutes on break and only a half an hour for lunch. Then back to the machine.

The main shift is swing shift and then the second shift is grave yard. If you have worked for long enough at the post office and quality for a day job and pass the memory test for all of the zip codes then you might be able to get a day shift. Only after several years of working at the post office.

As you probably know, Christmas time is a time that everyone will work ten to twelve hour shifts night after night. During this time you will be lucky to get a day off. Many times we would work twelve hours a night each night for a week. We would get very worn out but when Christmas time is in the air, it is a very special time, at least for a while, usually the beginning of the season.

We got to know each other very well. We became like family because we spend most of our time together working so hard. We learned each other's likes and dislikes. We learned each other's life styles and families, husbands, wives and the difficulties that they were going through at home. Who had a happy marriage and who did not? Then we could see who was interested in sleeping with whom. Who keep trying to get people to go to bed with them? I saw many affairs get started and went on for along time. Some of them did not hide it what so ever.

Then after about nine months after we became Letter Sorting Machine clerks it came time for us to bid on crews. You could stay where you were or try to get a gravy yard shift or an early afternoon shift with one of the other crews. If we chose to do this, we then would have to memorize many zip codes per that city or state codes that we had to memorize and take a test to be able to pass and be on that crew. It was all in the memorizing all the numbers.

Most of us went onto biding onto a crew and then therefore, we had then three months to memorize all the codes before the test. I moved to grave yard shift. Graveyard hours were from 10:30 p.m. to 7 a.m. or 9 a.m. with over time. It was a really hard shift for me. Some of us were dragging around 6 a.m. and we just wanted to go home. There were about four machines running almost all of the night. They all where running different schemes, these schemes where different codes for the different parts of the United States mail and also for the local main of the counties of the city in which I worked. We would have to memorize a two-digit code for the different part of the city so then the piece of mail would go to the right carrier. So then when that carrier would come in, first thing in the morning then that piece of mail would be in the tray waiting for the carrier to put it in order in his case then the carrier would pull out the mail from his case in route order for delivery.

We also would work on the OCR machines. This is a machine that would organize all the mail that came in from the mailboxes on the sidewalks where the general public dropped their mail. We then would pull that bring it to the main post office and have it go through this machine. Then it would speed through to the right area, whether it be a city or a state and then a clerk would go over to that bin and take all of the mail out of that bin and put it into a tray and send it off to the conveyer belt to go to the truck dock. This machine would read the zip code and put a special barcode mark on the bottom of the letter. Every large post office has these machines now. This machine does get the most mail moved in a timely order to where it is to go.

The mail processing clerks job on this machine is very difficult. You are constantly moving and going from this side to that side because the bins are all filling up at the same time and if they get to full it will stop the machine. The Forman of the shift is relaying on getting as much mail through that machine and if you have not done a good job, you should be ready to get a talking too. Each machine usually has two people running it. The person loading the machine. This person will have containers full of first class mail to go through this machine, one tray right after another and must always keep it going. Then the other person is the one running from one side to the other side. This machine, I believe to be the most difficult one to work on. You do not have a chance to stop and go to the bathroom. You do not have a chance to get something to drink or eat while you are working on this machine.

The time your break time comes around you are really ready for it. The only other time on this machine when you may have a little break is when the machine gets jammed up with a piece of mail that stops the whole machine. Unfortunately, a piece of mail is bent or part of the envelope is damaged but we will then put it in a plastic envelope and move it to its destination. We always do our best to get the mail moved to the right place. The trays of mail do weigh about ten to fifteen pounds apiece. This is where we usually get lots of exercise from moving and loading these trays up each and every day.

Each container holds seventy to seventy five trays. So every day, especially Christmas time we had to move the mail and get all those cards delivered to their families and friends.

At Christmas time, there was no time to be sick, no time to be injured and especially no time to stay at home and get well. They needed each and every body there and get as much mail done and as quickly as possible. Many times I had to work twelve hours. Boy was I tired by the time I went home. During those times that I worked graveyard, my children were very little and I would have to take them to school or daycare. I would drive them to school and I would stop at the traffic lights in the morning and tell them please wake me up when the light turns green. I would go into a little sleep time while I was behind the steering wheel of the car while the car was waiting at a stop light. My children would always wake me up and I was told to drive down the street. I did a good job. I drove safely.

I was so worn out that I chose to sleep more then to eat. I lost weight and sleep meant more to me then eating. I would eat lunch at the post office. I then relied on coffee to keep me going through the shift. To this day, I do not think I could work graveyard again. It was way to hard on my body and I think it is very difficult for the family and a person's body to work that shift.

I am very grateful for the people that do work that shift because I know what they are putting themselves through. As well as their family going through the problems of a tired spouse and not having time with there children because of having a job that ministers to the public. They do get a great job done during those hours.

One of the jobs that I put into was to work on one of the Letter Sorting Machine crews that worked from 10:30 p.m. to 7 a.m. I only did this because it was graveyard shift and I would make more money and by passing the test of memorizing 1900 items of zip codes and passing the test then I would be able to have two good days off together. I thought it was a good plan. I took the chance to get onto this crew. It was a very hard scheme to learn. I began to have trouble learning and memorizing it. I was having trouble so I made cards to study by. I needed to do this to pass the final test.

Each night at work, we would get only one hour to come into the computer room and work on the memorizing of the numbers for that crew and see how well I did for that hour. Well, I wasn't doing so well. I began to worry. I needed to do this because I wasn't sure I would be able to go back to my old job. I had to get serious and study. It isn't easy thing to do, when you have a husband and you're the one that takes care of everything, such as bills, cleaning the home and trying to get some sleep before going back to work.

Chapter Two
The Machine Supervisors

After about eight months of working at this post office, our crew met, Al Knight. He was an older man and seemed to be an Italian man with black hair and olive green eyes.

He had about four adult children at this time and a wife with whom he was married to all his adult life. He was a hard workingman and really loved his children. He was the only really devoted man and caring individual that was in the supervisory field at this post office. He would operate the large Letter Sorting Machines and the full crew of twelve to fourteen people that it took to run it and get the mail done through this machine.

I remember one night that I was working swing shift. It was about nine p.m. and I had this strange feeling come over me. I was just working and cleaning the mail out from the back of the machine and then went around the front to sit down and start keying the zip codes into the machine per piece of each mail that I saw go through the machine. I could not shake this bad feeling off. It kept coming to me that my mother, who I have, not spoke to for about two months, because she would not answer my calls. I had the feeling that my mother was trying to commit suicide. I knew that my little brother was there at the house. I knew that if anything was to happen, he was right there to help with this situation. I also knew that I was the one to stop her in the past from committing suicide when I lived at home.

I kept having this feeling that something was going on. So, after an hour of feeling this way. I went up to Al and told him, I have been having this feeling that something is wrong. I explained that my mother is an alcoholic and has tried to commit suicide before and I cannot stop this feeling. Can I go and see if she is all right and because my little brother would need some help and find out if she was trying to do this? I did not know what he would say because we were never to leave the post office. We needed to get the mail out.

I waited for about one minute for his response. He said, sure go ahead and go, but if things are all right, come right back as soon as possible, ok? I said, yes, I would be right back, thank you so much for letting me go. So I went and clocked out at the time clock and went to get my purse and jacket and off I went to the bad side of town where my mother and little brother were living and wondered, God why was I feeling this about my mom? Will I would look and see that everything was ok or will I find something wrong. Would I look like a fool to my mother when I pull into the driveway at nine thirty at night and ask if they are ok? What will they think if things are ok? I knew that I could not stay and visit because I would need to get right back at work and let Al know that everything was ok. This is all that went through my mind on the way there.

Ok, so here I am pulling into they're driveway and going up to the door. My little brother answers the door. Anthony, is everything ok? No, mom tried to commit suicide tonight. She tried to take a whole bottle of pills and she was drinking. I said oh no, our you ok? He said yes, a little shook up but I am ok. What brought you over here? I explained to him, I had this funny feeling at work that something was going on here at the house concerning mom. I just could not stop the feeling like she wanted to dye. I could also feel that you where here and were needing help with her. Isn't that strange.

Anthony said that she had thrown up all of the pills right before I got there and she was ok now and in bed sleeping. I knew that I should not go in and see her because when she drinks she could get very angry. The best thing to do was to just let her sleep.

I felt so sorry for my brother, Anthony. To leave him they're to have to go through the same types of things that I had to go through. I was so proud of him for knowing the right things to do. She would of died if it wasn't for his quick thinking. I told him, brother I love you so much but I have to get back to work. I told the boss that I felt like something was wrong and he said to go but get back as soon as possible.

He said, thanks for coming sis when you felt like this. I was so glad to see you. I am just going to go to bed myself. It has been quite a night. She hopefully will stay asleep though the night. I am going to turn all the lights off and lock the doors and then go to bed, you get back to work. Ok, brother, I will talk to you soon about this and how she acts after all this, ok? I answered, Ok. I love you brother and I will talk with you soon. Bye.

Off I went back to work. Clocked back into the building and then told Al, I am back, who was standing by the machine? He said to me, well, what did you find out? Yes, she was trying to commit suicide and my brother stopped her. I am glad that you went and your brother stopped her from death. I said so was I?

I turned around and went to the machine and sat down to key the mail to the right place. I figured that God must have wanted me to be there and help my brother. To this day I wonder why he let me know what was going on.

One of the nicest lady supervisors that I ever met was, Wanda. She was an older lady in her sixties. She had dark hair and her face had looked like she was through many hard things in her life. There were so many wrinkles on her face.

I wondered about her life for a long time. She treated me so nice every time she saw me. So one day after working with her for about three years I asked her about her life and her children? She said, well for most of my life from age of twenty-one I was an alcoholic and have been dry now for about five years. I feel so much better; I was bad here, at the post office. I would come in so drunk. They finally after a year of it said, you better get some help or you will lose your job. So I got help but then fell off of the wagon about a year and a half later. Then they gave me two weeks leave of absence and said, please don't let it happen again.

I then started to go to meetings and I have been dry every since. I feel so much better. I still think of drinking but I stop at that thought and realize just what that drink did to me. I lost my husband to divorce because of it and my kids, which I had three sons and one girl all went with their father and I stayed and drank. I see my children once in a while and they love me, and don't hold it against me. Their father was a good man and he put the right values into there hearts. I am so grateful for that. Now I have this job and soon I will be retiring and try to enjoy the rest of my life away from here. I am not sure what I will be doing but I will be doing it without drinking that is for darn sure.

I told her that I came from a very bad childhood and living with an alcoholic mother and how it was hard to go through but God got me throw it and He is the only reason that I did not turn into one or a drug user and also become a prostitute on the streets. She said well, keep the Lord in your life, He will show you the way. He has me.

Then we saw the big bosses coming off of the elevators so I said, well I guess I better get back to work, she said yes I guess so. It was good talking with you. She said the same.

There was one supervisor that many of us will never forget. His name was Bill T. He was one of a kind of men. He was the most awful person to work for; he was so angry and seems to hate life so much that most of us felt so sorry for him.

Bill would be the supervisor that we would need to work for when the machines went down and they needed us to do some kind of mail processing instead of just having us standing around. They would send us to the bottom floor of this post office and have us work on sorting the flat mail.

Bill was in charge of this department. He once was a machines supervisor but I was told he could not relate well with the machine clerks and therefore they put him on this floor to take care of this area. This was also good for him because he did not lose his supervisor position.

He did not get along with almost everyone. We believe that he was going through a bad divorce and this is why he was the way he was with all of us mail processing clerks.

We tried to stay out of his way. We did not want to ask him any questions in less we really needed to know the answer and had no other resource to get this answer.

Bill would yell at you for coming up to him. He would say why are you out of your case and it better be a good question for you not throwing that mail in your case? Most of us would take a deep breath before coming up to him.

He made so many men mad at him. He had many enemies. During the time that I was at that post office, I remember hearing of a couple death treats to Bill. Then his car was also damaged four times during that time.

He was also beat up one evening after work. He always parked his car on the local streets surrounding that post office and would have it in a different place each night but during this particular evening it did not help him. He was being watched by these two men. They watched him walk out of the post office and waited until he was almost to his car. Unfortunately for Bill he parked near railroad tracks and was pretty much all alone where no one could hear any noises or see what was about to happen.

These men went ahead and grabbed him and just started to beat him over and over again until he could not get up. Then they went ahead and damaged he car again. I guess his was in bad shape. No one would tell me who these men where. They did say that they wore masks and ball caps and where dressed in dark clothing.

Bill did not come back to work for about a week. The one's that heard about Bill and cared for him as a human being felt sorry for him. We knew that because of his anger and how he treated people is why he experienced this.

He never did change for about three years after this. After three years he did get remarried and began to become a human being again. He was claim and treated people the way he should of and was a better supervisor.

It was spring time while the group of us which was about fifteen people worked together in this particular building and in this building there was an older man and a older woman that I worked closely with. Then behind us was twelve other people that did there job throwing mail and taking care of whatever needed to be done on the floor that day.

In the last year I was able to learn many things of the mail processing at this location because whenever you go to a new post office or go as a detail job to work there for a known or unknown period of time, you must therefore learn the zip codes and where each piece of mail goes to. Each carrier has their own route and say about 1800, pieces of mail on their route to deliver too.

When a clerk comes in they must learn the street address where this piece of mail will go to which carrier and then into the slot for that carrier so then they can come and get there mail during the morning hours and start by putting it into the delivery sequence for their delivery on the route.

It all starts with the mail sorting clerk. This is so important and must be done very fast. A mail sorting clerk must get to the post office about four to five a.m. and begin by getting the trays of mail and sit down and begin to sort away until all the mail is done. We needed to make sure that all the carriers have all of the mail for that day included third class mail.

Once the first class mail has been sorted, and then after a fifteen minute break, we then come back to the spot where we were sorting and begin to sort the third class mail until all of that is done. We need to be done as early as ten o'clock in the morning. Most of the carriers are ready to leave about ten o'clock and have started to pack the mail into their mail jeep or mail car.

Once all of the mail has been worked up we then move onto the front counter and get ready to open up the front counter for the customers that buy stamps and also wanting to send packages and certified letters. In my opinion, money orders are a very good idea to buy through the post office.

Well, I was able to work side by side of an older lady, by the name of Linda and got to know her life some. We shared many things that we had in common and enjoyed working next to each other while working the letter mail up for the carriers. I could tell that she did not open herself up to many people and she did not like many of the people in this office, I asked her how long have you been working in this office? She said that she had been here for about three years now and it was an ok office to work in.

She began to tell me about the main sorting woman, by the name of Sue. Linda said that she got to know Sue a little bit by sorting next to her and that Sue like to talk a lot. She said that Sue would ask many questions each and every day and always wanting to know things that has happened in my life. Linda said that it got to be brothersome to sit and have someone ask questions about my past each and every day. Linda said, I just got to the point that I just did not answer her questions anymore and finally had to say to her stop asking me. I do not want to tell you anymore about my life, do you understand that? She said, Sue said, yes I understand and no more questions.

So then I could see that in a way they were enemies. They did not talk to each other unless one of them really needed to know something about work. They stay in their department and just did there job.

Here I come on the scene now and start my letter throwing with Linda. She tells me many things about her life and I did not really ask any questions, she just told me.

I felt then that we had many things in common except that she was about twelve years older then I was. We had many things in common like she had a husband die a few years ago and I just went through having a husband die.

She enjoyed our time together and so did I. Before I knew it we were working side by side in our work station most of the time. I really liked her and thought she was a good worker.

Then she began to have some personal problems and then some physical problems. She came to work anyway. She was in severe pain but she would just slow down and work, but she made it in most of the time.

I am not sure what caused some of her moods to change after this period of time. I wonder if it just was her physical body hurting or just the people in the post office that got on her nerves but then she changed in attitude.

Her attitude and mood changed. She began to get so moody and did not like being around anyone. She started to work quite slower then she was. I tried to ask her what was going on but she would not tell me.

Then about three months later, she began to whistle and whistle louder. Her whistle was so annoying and made it hard to work and then she got where she would whistle all day long.

Then Sue came up to me one day. She said, Carolyn would you please ask her to stop whistling. We all want her to stop whistling, we can not take it anymore. We are not sure why she is doing it but I know that if I asked her to stop, she would not stop, she would just whistle louder. You seem to get along with her well, can you talk to her about stopping her whistling? I told her, yes I can try but I don't know if she will listen to me.

So one afternoon, I asked her, why are you whistling so much these last few days? She said that she just likes to whistle and thought that she would do it here. I told her that it was disturbing some of the other peoples work and they were wondering if you could please stop.

She then got so angry and just started to whistle even louder. I told Sue when Linda was not around that I did try but it did not work, sorry. It looks like it has made things even worse.

So in the meantime, I still worked around Linda each and everyday after that and yes, she would whistle as loud as she could even around me. I began to wonder why, this is taking energy and why was she doing this. She never told anyone apparently why she was doing this. After about two more weeks of this noise I went to the supervisor and asked him if he could talk with her about stopping her whistling.

This supervisor was very reluctant to speck with her. He did not want to get involved in her moods and the problems on the floor with anyone of his crew that he had to supervise. I could understand that but I came to a point that I could not deal with the noise any longer and I knew that everyone else felt the same.

He then finally went and talked with her and asked her to stop whistling. He told her it was too much noise and the customers were being bothered by her whistling. So when he told me what all he said, I thought ok then today things will be much better and then all of us will have a better working inviroment atmoshere here at work. Great I felt better and said thank you to him.

Linda came on duty that day after I was at work for about two hours. I smiled at her and said, "Good Morning" to her. She said, "Good Morning" back to me and then came around to where I was working. Then after being on duty for five minutes, she began whistling very loud. I thought to myself, what is she doing. She can not be doing this after the supervisor told her not to do it any longer. The supervisor could then write her up with a letter of warning for going against what he asked her to do. Why was she continuing to do this?

Linda kept doing this for the next five days. I finally went back to the supervisor and said. I thought that you talked with her. He said, I did talk with her. She is just doing this on her own and has not listened to what I have asked of her.

He then said, I will wait a little while longer and see if she stops doing it. Then I might go back and ask her again. I said, good I hope you do. It is really hard to work and do a good job around this noise.

Two weeks have gone by, and she is still whistling. I waited and waited for it to stop. Nothing, she still continues.

I then said to myself, ok it is up to me to handled this problem on my own. I realized that the supervisor were not going to do anything about this problem. He did not want to get involved and have her treat him badly. So I thought ok what can I do?

I asked her one more time, could you please stop whistling for me. She would not. The other people that was working in the building began to wear ear pugs in their ears. They did this each and everyday.

I thought that this is like a form of harrasment. She is doing this just to get on the nerves of everyone in this building. I do not know why, but she realizes that she is disturbing everyone and she has made up her mind this is what she will do each and everyday, while she is here at work.

Ok then, I thought about the people that had suffered many things in their lives. I thought you know that people from many different times of history, such as African American people that suffered wrong treatment and torcher that they never did anything to deserved that type of treatment but by the color of there skin they were treated that way. That was so wrong.

Then I remember how they just handled it and made it through it and came back to there family at the end of the day and made the best of it, each and everyday.

I then thought of another situation that people had to go through. I thought of the concentration camps. How the Jews where killed and the treatment that they went through. I began to think how did they handle not eating. How they handled there minds and was able to not say anything and deal with the attitudes of the German soldiers. For example, how the woman handled it mentally while they were being rapped by the soldiers and not make any angry faces or attitudes towards them while they were doing that terrible thing to them. I know that these women knew that if they made any facial attitudes on there face that the soliders would kill them right then and there.

CHAPTER THREE
AFTER HOURS

Our Machine group had been working very hard this last week, it has been another 10 hours shift, so one of the gays, Jesse mentioned about going over to Champions Tavern across the street from the Post Office after work. So we all started to pass the message to go over there after work, after all we got off at 11:30 p.m. and we could relax a little before going home.

It was a little bar, just a small little dance floor but once in awhile we would use it, especially if we had a few drinks and felt great. This bar had a lot drugs passing through it, I never part-took of the substance but many people did, especially my friend Betsy. She used to do allot of drugs because of being a small town girl from Iowa. She would show her independence in a quite way.

What surprised me the most of the supervisors and the general Forman that came in and drank and laughed at the next two tables away from us, what surprised me the most was that they did the hard drugs and how they would make eyes at the chosen woman that they wanted. They looked at me a little, but I was to busy having some fun with my friends and knew that I needed to go home because tomorrow was another day. I never could drink very much so I limited myself.

We would go out once in a while when we could. We even went to a strip place once for the men in our group. Some of us women, including myself were shocked at what a woman had to do to get some money. We did not stay there at that location for very long. We just pick up and went to another dancing location where there was a band. We all like listening to a live band.

We of course, would leave about 2:30 a.m. in the morning and come back to work the next day about 2:30 p.m. to work on the letter storing machines. Some of us had a headache like me but we did our jobs.

Many people wanted to get hooked up but it did not happen because they were married.

Some of the mail handlers would come into work and already be drunk and then leave after there shift and go right back to the same bar. I just could not see how they did that.

We would see the same old supervisors in the bar or as we drove pass the bar to get onto the freeway to get home, we would see that, oh what's his name was in the bar all day again and he will not be in good shape at work that night.

More then drinking went on. Most of the single people got to know one another because the only time they had to socialize was at the post office.

Then there were several people that got a divorce and found someone at the post office and started to date them and before you knew it, they were together as a couple. You would see them walk down the main hall together and inside the post office you could hold hands and walk around only when you were on break or going to lunch.

Then most of those couples were announcing that they were getting married. This was a good thing because they could carpool and take care of each other. They would always see one another at the post office and there was a 90% chance that their marriage was not going to end in divorce because of never seeing your spouse cause of the hours that you had to work.

Most of us new career postal service people stop running around once we were given a new shift and position on a machine because we had a real life now and wanted to do a good job at it. So that broke up our after hours group.

CHAPTER FOUR
THE CRAZY CARRIER

I have worked in many different locations. A large post office to a very small post office has a Postmaster who is in charge of the facility and the people who work at that location. It is a very large responsibility to take on because you need to make sure that you keep all the mail secure and that each day except Sundays of course, gets delivered even in bad weather. The clerks and the carriers need to be there to do the job other wise it is the job of the Postmaster to make sure the mail has been delivered for that day. Then do all of the paperwork that is required and make sure the hours of duty time is not going over for the amount given for the clerks and carriers.

This can be a very complex position. I had the chance to fill in for a Postmaster once, while she was away on a trip. I enjoyed it but I realized that there was more to it then I had previously thought.

When I met her was in November. I was moving into this town with my new husband. It was a very small town and I believed at the time they had about 12,000 people that lived in this town. This was a very small post office only had one and a half carriers to do the delivery routes. What I mean by one and a half of a carrier is, another carrier would come in and work only two hours or so sorting the mail inside the post office and then deliver that mail on this route. It would only take that person about four hours instead of the normal delivery time of eight, ten or even twelve hours to deliver the mail. It all depends on the city or town as to how many hours it will take to deliver.

This town was not large, I was working in a very large populated area before this and now I have transferred into this very small town as the new clerk of this post office. I would work only about six hours a day. I needed to make sure that I had all the mail sorted and put into the post office boxes so that people could get their mail by 10:00 a.m. and everything else needed to be done by noon. I would work as fast as possible and get the job done so I would have the rest of the day off before my children would get out of school and then be able to cook dinner for my husband and children and then off to bed because getting up at 3:30 a.m. to go to work was very early for me.

My husband would get the kids up and then get them to the bus and then himself off to work and then home about 6:30 p.m.

Living in a very small town was a learning experience for me as well. This small town was a very close net town. If you were not born and raised in this town, you really where not the same kind of person as they are. You then were an outsider. I did not mind it, I was just me.

Many things I saw in this post office. I would see customers in the early morning come in that was drunk. I would see very rich people coming in to get their mail. I would see people that worked for the Forest Service Department. I would see people that were high on drugs. I would see many people with several fingers missing and on they're way in to work, to work hard all day. People of that town would come into the post office to say; have you heard what is going on now with so and so. There were many woman and men who was outstanding people. Very many of them were caring and willing to help those around the community of this small town. I just tried to stay away from the ones that thought that they owned this town. If I started a relationship with them, it did come to an end.

I was working in this post office and after about a month of working, I had to work closely with the main carrier. She would come in every morning about 6:00 a.m. and I would hear her unlocking the back door and then see would walk in. She immediately would go to the case were I had put mail that I had just sorted on her case so that when she would come in, she had work to do.

Well, she was an older woman and apparently she had been working at this location for about twelve years. She had her job down pat. She was the best.

She would come in and I would say, "Good Morning," to her. She would only say, "Good Morning," to me only about four times during the two and a half years that I worked in the post office.

She was very quiet most all of the time. She would move around quickly in her case. She became different from one day to the next. I would come in and wonder what she would be like this morning. I wanted to know what was wrong with her?

I would come in each day after that and would wonder just what was going to happen today? I came in and just did my work of getting the mail and packages all worked up first because I was not sure what she would be like. I made sure that it was done as soon as possible because the day after a holiday she started to come in earlier and I just did not want to deal with her. It was scary when you are not sure what a person is all about and why they do the things they do. I asked the Postmaster why was the main carrier like she is? What made her do the things that she does first thing in the morning? I told her what I saw that she had did and I just had no reason why and just wanted to know, if she knew why.

The Postmaster said, she has acted like this for years, we think that she has had a nervous breakdown and not sure what has caused it but she has been strange for years now. Just keep to yourself and she will leave you alone. I would not talk to her in the mornings, she said to me.

So that is just what I did in the mornings, I keep to myself and just did my work.

About a month later when it was wintertime, I came in as usual and did my work. All of a sudden, I heard the back door unlock, it scared me at first, and then I realized that it must be the main carrier. I listened, she unlocked the door all right but she just stood there at the door with the door open for about five minutes and then came in. She was in between the wall the entrance way, but not into the main part of the building. She just stood about five feet away from the entrance of the main part of the building. I wondered why was she doing this? She was next to the cart where I put her packages on; these packages are for her to deliver on her route. She then stood by the cart where her packages where.

All of sudden, she started to hit the packages and then throw the packages off of the cart. I had no idea why she was doing this. I just did not know what to do? Should I go over and ask her what are you doing? Should I stay put and not say anything and pretend not to see it? Should I not say anything to her while I am here? I just did not know what to do. I thought to myself I better just stand here and keep putting the mail into the case and not let her see that she is making me feel uncomfortable or nervous or let her see that she is making me scared. I do not know if she could become physical with me. I do know that a crazy person can have enormous strength and I did not want to get her mad by any means. I was quite smaller then she is.

I mentioned it to the Postmaster, that once again I witnessed this particular morning and if she knew what all of that was about. She said, sometimes she will do this, and try not to let it get to you. I would watch her and just do my job and get out of that post office as soon as I could.

She then started to do more and more strange things. She truly was a disturbing woman. I could just see that her mental health was not good. I was so careful what I did in the mornings and watched every move that she made. I had a crazy, unhealthy mother and knew what she was capable of doing, for example my mother threw me down to the ground and pounded my head into the floor and I could not get her off of me with all the strength that I had, I could not get her off.

So I knew that she was taller and probably stronger. She was a single woman that had two grown children and was helping them out financially and worked at this post office for a long time but something was making her go insane. I did not want to be the item that took her over the edge.

About five months later, she was, on some days acting as normal as anyone could be. But, she would not talk; only time that she would talk was to ask me a question about the mail that she absolutely needed to know. Otherwise, no conversation at all. On the other days, it was back to strange behavior and just doing her work. She made me take measures to protect myself. For example, I needed to use a middle size knife to open the mail boxes so I could sort the mail and then I would put it along side my case so if I needed to use it again, it would be right there. If I knew that she was going to come around my case for any reason at all, such as to go to the bathroom or something to get that she needed to prepare the mail for delivery, then I would immediately pick up the knife and put it into the drawer right under me, so that she would not see that I had a knife and possible try to use it on me.

She seemed, as the months grew longer that she was not getting any better. I worried more and more about her condition. I did not say anything because I knew the Postmaster and the part time sub carrier could see it too. We did not know what to do.

The Postmaster told me, when it was just us two in the room and no one else could hear what we were saying. She told me of the odd behavior things that she was doing like; the carrier would deliver her route but on this day she would deliver ¾ of her route and then just stop delivering and bring back the rest of the mail from her car. She would not deliver all of her routes mail. She just came in and put the mail back on her desk and just lifted the building. She did not say a word to the Postmaster or call the other sub for help on the route so all the community would receive there mail for the day.

Later the Postmaster found out that she just stop delivery the mail without saying anything to anyone and then just went home. Nobody knew why? The Postmaster had to ask her why she did such a thing on the previous day, then the carrier got mad and said: You have no right to ask me this question. The Postmaster did not know what to do. She had to take this problem to a higher source. She then needed to call and speck to the division manager of all the post office buildings. He handled all problems with carriers, clerks and mail handlers. This manager was whom the Postmaster's went to if there was any trouble in their office. He then said, she was the acting Postmaster at this office and that she must give the carrier a letter stating that she must go to a doctor and then return after a one-week medical leave of absence. She must bring back a slip from her doctor that she is able to perform her duties as a carrier of the United States Postal Service.

The Postmaster typed up this letter and then sent it to her house. She freaked out and was yelling and saying all kinds of bad words to the Postmaster and then left the building and slammed the back door.

We did not see her for the rest of that week and half of the next week. It was so peaceful and pleasant to go to work and not have to worry while I was working. I had my own things to worry about in life and to try to get all the mail done and take care of all my duties within the hours that I must get them done within.

I could see that everyone was on edge working in this office with this crazy carrier. That is the name that we all gave her: The Crazy Carrier.

After about two weeks, she then came back to the post office and opened the back door. The Postmaster was so nice and warned me that tomorrow she should be coming back and so just take it easy with her and just do your job and leave her alone, ok. I said, oh yes, I would be quite and just do my own work.

It's the next morning, oh, I can hear that she is now at the back door, I quickly take a deep breath, and here we go. I need to look like nothing has happened. I need not make her mad for any reason, be cool Carolyn, you can do it.

She came in to the main area and looked around. She then picked up a tray of mail and slammed it down on her counter. She then started to put the mail into the slots and she would do this like she was extremely anger. We would call that throwing the mail into the case.

I did not move her way. I made sure not to look at her and just do my work. She did not speck to me at all. Then the Postmaster came in. The crazy carrier then spoke to her and said in a very matter of fact way to the Postmaster, here is the letter from the doctor that you and the son of bitch manager said that I must bring back upon my returning to work.

Of course, by the law the note from the doctor could not tell anyone what her medical condition was. It would only say that she was able to perform the duties of her job. It did say so, the Postmaster said to me after she had left to do her route.

It was starting to take a toll on me; I was becoming very stress out myself. I then just tried to let it all go once I was done working and was home. Just another day working in the post office.

The crazy carrier then after about six months later started to get angry again. She would go to the bathroom and slam the bathroom door. She would come inside from the back door and see the packages and get down on one knee and start throwing the packages off of the cart that I had just put them onto. They were sorted by me for her route. I guess they were not in right order or something like that. I just did not know, she did not say and I was not sure if I should ask, so I did not say a word.

Then one day, it was springtime now. The crazy carrier did not seem to be angry during this time. She was not so bad but was still doing the normal crazy kind of things.

Then one day, she did not come into work. I had to call the Postmaster at home when the carrier did not come in by 6:30 a.m. Whenever the carrier or clerk was not there to work, the Postmaster needs to know because someone has to do the delivery or sort the mail so we can get it out to the people.

The Postmaster came immediately into the office. She then tried and tried to call the carrier to find out why she was not in. No answer on her phone. Then the Postmaster had no choice but to call the part time carrier and see if she could come in and do both routes that day. She would get over time. We were not to get over time, but in this case it would have to be ok. She called the part time carrier and she said, she would be right in. She was able to get all the mail delivered that day. The next day came around, still no sign of the regular carrier, no calls, no answers why she was not they're to work.

The Postmaster, once again, had to call the division manager at the main office and ask him what should she do. He told her, she had no choice but to have the part time carrier to take over the route yesterday. Postmaster said that the part time carrier did a good job but also got paid overtime because there was no other person to do this job. He said, make sure that the part time carrier can take over that route until we find out what is going on and if you need to hire another part time carrier. If you need to, go ahead and hire another part time carrier. Have your clerk available to take over the office duties if you need to go out to deliver some of the mail. She said, ok, I can do this and to keep him posted of any new details.

Well, four months had pasted and still no word from the crazy carrier. We all wondered if she had committed suicide or just had another nervous breakdown.

The part time carrier was getting pretty tired of doing the main carriers work. She was ready to take over the job but needed to get better daycare for her children. The Postmaster had to send out four certified return receipt letters to the carriers home for her to read, stating that if you do not come back to work, your job will be endanger and that you had thirty days to reply or four fit your job.

The Postmaster never did get a receipt back from the certified return receipt letters that she mailed out. The part time carrier would go by her house everyday and said that she saw her vehicle by her house but did not see her. Then the carrier said, that she would drive by her house at night and that she could see that the lights were on. We were very worried about her condition.

Well, after about two more weeks we found out that the crazy carrier had called the main office and spoke with the Head Postmaster of the main office about her situation and that she was not coming back.

The crazy carrier said that it was the entire Postmasters fault. She was the reason that she cannot come back to work their. She is the reason that she is so emotionally upset and feel like she has had a nervous breakdown. She would take her retirement had have nothing to do with the postal service again. That is all she said.

Well, the Postmaster of that office hired the part time carrier for that position and went from there. Things became much better in the office. The crazy carrier was the talk of the town for a long time. People would say that they would see her in town getting some food once in awhile. They believed that her grown children were having trouble with the law and all of that was making her go crazy because they needed some financial help from her and the pressure was to much for her to bare. She just could not take it any longer.

I really do believe that she was possibly able of hurting me or one of the other people in that office. I did fear for my life and never want to go through that again.

This Postmaster was a matter of fact, sweet and very hard working Postmaster that took pride in doing the best job that she could do. This Postmaster has been the Postmaster of this small office for twenty years and has helped the community in anyway that she could. She would clean, she would let people put up messages on the wall in the outer area where the doors to the post office boxes were. People looking for babysitters or needing a part time job.

This Postmaster would help by collecting cans of food for the needed. She would go pick up the bags of food that people would leave at there doors for the carrier to pick up, the carrier's car was not large enough to hold all the food so then the Postmaster would take it upon herself to go out and leave me in the office to take care of the customers while she went to pick up the bags of food. I thought that it was very nice of the Postmaster to do that; she did not have to take that part of the carrier's job because this was designed for only carriers to do. But, she took it on herself to help the carrier and also because she knew that the carrier had many things to do now that she is doing a full time carriers job.

CHAPTER FIVE
THE BLUE ROOM

Well, I was working on the Letter Sorting Machines number three and I was five minutes late from lunch. I went out for lunch and went down the street to get a sandwich at the nearby store. I really had to hurry because I needed to go down the post office stairs and then go to my car. I had to hurry and get lunch and drive back trying to eat while I am driving and on my way back to the post office building, then up the stairs and get to the time clock and punch into the time clock on time. I needed to do my best to get back right on time.

So unfortunately, I was late five minutes. I was hoping that I would not hear anything about being five minutes late but I was around the back of the machine and here comes the supervisor as I was coming around the front to sit down and start typing the zip codes for my half an hour. The supervisor of the machine said, Carolyn, I want you to report to the Blue Room in the office right away. I said, ok. I had to clock off the machine and walk to the main office and go into the Blue Room.

The Blue Room consists of a room off from the main part of the main office on the workroom floor, usually the second floor where the superintendent's office is. It is a room that has been painted all blue, on all of the walls in this room. It has a large table in the middle of the room and a chair on both sides of the table.

The idea of the supervisor or the superintendent to have you come into this room and sit there without anyone by your side and listen to them but you out and tell you what a bad job you have been doing and you better never do that again. If you do chose to do this again, you will be suspended and the third time this happens you will be let go, your job will come to an end.

If you do try to say something, they usually will tell you to keep your mouth shut. You listen to me and listen well. I listened and just said fine, I will not be late again. Then as I was leaving the room, I laughed, I thought what a barbaric way of talking to someone about being late.

What happened to being good at communication, where two people could come together and talk about things in a decent way and meet each other half way?

I felt as though I was in prison and I better watch every step I made in the building because I could be fired for any little thing which I might do wrong. It was a joke, a bad joke on us employee's who really tried to do a good job. I had worked there now for four years and was not late coming back from lunch often, about three times in four years.

Come to find out about a year later that this supervisor was interested in me for a sexual relationship. I had no idea why he really had me go into the Blue Room the year before. He was married but was always in a bad mood. We just thought that his sex life with his wife was not going very well and he had pint up emotions as a man will get and he was taking it all out on us.

After working there for four and a half years, our crew of twelve people on the letter sorting machines got to know each other pretty good and now and then go out to the local bar or someone's home to have a drink or two and then go home. This is how some of the single people got to know each other.

Well, that particular supervisor was on our letter-sorting machine at that time and so was Linda who was an older woman in her forties and she was a widow at this time because her husband died. She wanted to have everyone come over to her house to have some drinks and food and have some fun. Only a few people knew that Linda's husband shot himself there in the front room of Linda's home.

Linda asked the supervisor if he wanted to come over to her home with all of us for a drink. He said maybe. At this time he was going through a divorce and did not seem so angry all of the time, he had some good days and some days you could see that he could blow at any minute.

We all stopped at a bar to have a couple of drinks in the local town where she lived and then went directly over to Linda's house. We were all there and then about thirty minutes later; there he was at the door. When we all looked at him, you could tell that he had a few drinks before he came over to her house. He then sat by me. I was a good-looking woman back then. I could see that he had a hard on.

Then before I knew it, other people could also see that he had a hard on. I did not know what to do. He kept looking at me and then he left to go to the bathroom. He came back and sat on the couch. We all had another drink and was talking and laughing and pretty soon he had another hard on, he started to move around in his set and before you knew it, his pants had ripped because of the extreme hard on. We all started to laugh. We did not mean too but we could not help it.

He got up and said he had to leave. I did not know what to say or think. I was still married at this time. I then knew that he was interested but stood my distance away from him. I knew I could not be with an angry man even if I was single.

CHAPTER SIX
ALCOHOL & DRUGS

The alcohol and the drugs were happening everywhere. From the first floor employees to the top floor of the post office building. Office people to the janitors that were cleaning the building. Don't get me wrong, it was not the general population of the people using, it was a few. For whatever reason they had for using, maybe to keep going on or to handle the job duties of the life of a postal career person. Who knows?

In fact, one of my experiences was one of my first dates after getting a divorce from my first husband. I was asked out on a date by a letter carrier and I thought he looked like a very nice man. He had a good job and he was single and I thought he and I had a lot in common. So he took me out for a very nice dinner and then he took me over to his house to have a drink, so I went with him.

I saw his home and talked with him for a while and then he reached over and kissed me and then he wanted to know if I want to spend the night with him. I told him I would think about it. So then it seemed like he let his hair down and I really got to see what he was all about. He became much more informal around me and said would you like to smoke some pot or do you do anything else? I told him no. He said, ok.

He then started to drink a few more drinks and then he smoked some pot and then he really started to talk. I found out all kinds of things about his life.

He then started to tell me that he is a heroin user and what kind of hi that gives him. He said he has been trying to get off of it but it is so hard. He said that when he has gotten off of it, he is locked in his home and he sweets and has sever stomach pain and just can not eat and he is no one to be around during that time. He also said, that he breaks a lot of things in his home. I felt so sorry for him, but I knew I needed to go. I did not want to get involved with a man that did that or any other type of drug. I thought smoking a little pot now and then was ok to relax but not a drug that controls a person and especially I knew I did not want anyone like that around my children, I wanted a wonderful role model and a hard working man to love and care for my kids.

He then drove me home after being at his house for about three hours and I got out and said thanks, and bye. I never called him back and he called me a couple of times but I never returned his phone call.

I often wondered what must have happened to him. Did he over dose himself? Did he get off of that drug? I was not able to get the newspaper because I was to busy working and raising kids and once I was done with household cores and the kids then it was time to go to work.

Then there was a middle-aged woman that started about three years after I did and she was a clerk. She was tall and wore the new aged culture type of clothing. I believed that she was trying to look younger, you know what I mean. She had a lot of make-up on and was not over weight but was not skinny. Her hair was dark brown and she looked as though she might have been around thirty-seven to forty years old.

I met her in the women's bathroom at the sink and she looked like she was sick. I asked her if she was ok? She said yes, just very sleepy. I said, I knew what she means. But she really looked whipped out to me. Then I could smell alcohol on her breath so then I thought to myself, she must have been out drinking all night and then came into work. The she said, she needed to go lay down in the woman's break room which is right behind the woman's bathroom. This is one of the only break rooms for women that has an old green long couch for women to come and lay down on. In all my years in the postal service, I have never seen such a nice break room-lounge area for women. I wished that most of the post offices would have this for women, especially when they are pregnant.

She asked me to wake her up in an hour, if I could come back into the break room and get her up. I was working only a little ways away from the woman's bathroom so I knew I could come back, I knew I would need to go to the bathroom again anyway so sure I will come back and wake you up.

If the supervisors would of known about this, we both would of gotten into big trouble. I wanted to give her a break and help her.

I came back and woke her up and then she got up and went out and she went back to work. I think she was working down stairs with the mail handlers. I really never did find out what her job was. So then about two days later I saw her again. In the woman's break room behind the bathroom in the woman's lounge area.

She was drunk, she could hardly walk. Her make-up was looking really bad. She was a mess. Then all of sudden, she had to run into the bathroom and throw up. I went in behind her and asked her if she was ok, she said yes.

CHAPTER SEVEN
PEOPLE WITH INJURIES

I have seen and talked with many of the people that have gotten physically hurt from working at one of the postal service facilities. Others that do not put in an accident report form are very scared to do so and just plain do not want something to happen to their job. They have a righteous fear, unfortunately

In all three-work positions where most of the work is done is, Mail handlers, Clerks and Letter Carrier. These areas of the mail sorting work is about 80% of all the mail processing and gets your mail and all of the corporations which includes the bulk mail out to where ever you want it to go. They work long hours and must, and I mean must be there everyday to do this process. No matter if you are extremely sick, just had a miscarriage, heartache, or hurt your leg or a migraine headache, you must come to work. I have personally seen this.

A very nice man that injured his spin by lifting at the post office lifting heavy boxes out from one of the trucks at the main postal facility office dock. He injured it so badly that he needed to be in bed on a board and only get up to do some exercise for his muscles and then back to ice and heat treatment before going back to bed. He spent about a week in the hospital before going home to recover. His time that he had worked at the post office without receiving an injury was about fifteen years. This was his first injury.

He then had to use all of his sick leave time that he had saved up so his family could receive income for that two-week period. Then next came his annual leave pay that he saved for vacation. He used all of what he had saved within about two months. This is money that his family could live on. They did not have a saving account saved up at this time. They used up what they had saved for previous emergency before this happened.

His wife did not have a job. She was a stay home wife. She then took care of him at home and they were wanting to start having children. He filed a claim for injury with his post office, but it was not granted to him, they felt that he lifted the wrong way. He then appealed the workman's compensation claim and tried again. He went into the interview and was asked all kinds of questions and he said it was recorded.

Well, about two months later, he heard back from the workman's compensation board. No, sorry we did not have well enough evidence to grant workman's compensation claim. He was outraged and he did not know what to do. He then told his wife, honey I think you will need to go out and look for work. She said, ok. She was able to get a position that paid $8.00 an hour.

This got medical bills paid so he could go to the doctor and get medication. But he said, we have no money for the house payment and food to eat. He said to his wife, the only blessing out of all of this is that we have no children at this time.

So about four months later, they lost their house. She had to get help to move everything because he was in no physical shape to help her and he felt so bad about it. They moved into a very small apartment. He then decided that he would try to go back to work at the post office and work with his pain and just not move very fast.

He humbly swallowed his pride and let it sink to the bottom of his stomach. So he came into the main office of the post office. He went into the office of the Postmaster and said, I would like to come back to work now. He said, no. You cannot come back to work without having a doctor's order that states you are completely better and physically able to perform the job duties of your position.

So then he went into see the doctor, he thought to himself, great another doctors bill I will have to pay just for having to get a medical release form so I can go back to work. The doctor looked at his back and did some test and said, I don't think so. You cannot even bin over to your knees. I legally cannot give you a medical release form so you can go back to work. I think that you would not even be able to go through a whole days work with the kind of work you would have to do. Then the doctor said, the release form was out of the question, sorry.

He came home and told his wife, we will have to try to get welfare or some kind of state assistance. He told her, I am so sorry for all of this. I did not want or mean to get hurt. I am so sorry for making your life so difficult and bad at this time.

She was depressed and sad for him but she tried hard not to show it, she just gave him a kiss and said, I love you and you are not the one to blame for all of this.

He then thought of the postal union. I will call and see if they will help me. I joined the union but stop my membership a few months before I got hurt, but I know that they said they would still help postal workers even if you do not pay for any membership in the union.

He called the next day. He called and they listened to him. The person on the phone said that they would look into the situation and get back with him. This gave him some hope. He was happy for the first time in two months. Then the call came in from the post office union. He told him that they have looked into the situation but unfortunately we cannot do anything to help you. You should have gotten in touch with us right after it happened. He said to him, I could not, I went directly to the hospital and then home to recover and this is where I have been until able to get in touch with you. He just said, sorry but there is nothing we can do for you.

He told his wife, the money I gave them was for nothing. He became depressed again. His wife tried hard not to show her depression. She would cry when he was not in the room and then cover it up so he would not see.

She then said to him, honey I can get another job. The mall is just across the street from the job place that I have now. They have a shoe store that is looking for someone. Remember, that I was a shoe salesperson before we got married. He said, yes I remember. But honey, I don't know if you can work all that hard. She said, I can do it honey. You have to just take care of yourself while I am gone at work until I can get home to take care of you, sweetheart.

He felt again, as if he has let his wife down, she has to work so hard to support us while I just sat at home doing nothing.

He began to suffer from depression after a year and a half because his doctor said you will not be able to lift anything over 20 lbs. For the rest of your life and you will be in some pain, I can give you pain medication but there will come a time that when you should think about having back surgery. If you have back surgery you will have a 50% chance of total recovery of your injuries. Would you like to go ahead with back surgery now? He said, no.

He talked it over with his wife and she also said no. She heard of people getting back surgery and the outcome is worse then before. He said, I have heard of that also, honey.

The post office accounting office called one day and wanted to know of what he wanted to do with his retirement fund. Was he going to come back and work? He felt like laughing. What a joke.

She wanted to know if he wanted to pull his retirement fund out? Did he want to add to the retirement fund each month? She needed to know what he wanted to do. He said, I couldn't come back to work. Doctor will not release me. She said, you would need to make up your

mind what you want us to do. He said, I would have to call you back. I
will talk with my wife. Ok, she said, I will hear back from you this week,
yes he said. He talked with his wife, what should we do honey? Should
I take it all out? If I do we will have to pay a penalty on it with the IRS.
I do not have enough years to get a monthly settlement where it will be
enough to live on per each month.

They decided to withdrawal all of his retirement and pay the penalty
to the IRS. After doing so, they ended up with $24,000 to live on. They
lost their house and also now they have bad credit for losing a house.
His wife said, honey we have bills that really needs to be paid. We are
late on the phone bill, the electric bill and the garbage bill is all late and
we hardly have any food to eat. He said, ok, lets get these bills paid off
and also get both of the cars tuned up because they are starting to have
mechanical problems and not running right. She said well, lets do that.
Before they knew it, there money was down to $17,000 dollars. He said,
we have to save the rest of our money in the bank in case of an emergency.
The next day, the main cars that she was driving blow a rod through
the engine. They needed to get another car. They bought an older car
for $3,500.00 and then after that there funds were even lower but they
needed a good running car for her.

About four months after that he decided, I will go into another post
office and see if I can go to work just as a casual worker, the kind that they
hire for just Christmas time. He would come in and do the grunt work
that they have only the casuals do. The Postmaster talked with him he
said that he worked for years but got this injury and now he is better and
can work. It seemed as if I had the worse record file on me, he looked at
me and said, I'm sorry but we have no position for you. Maybe you can
get a position at another post office. Have a good day.

He said, I know that men should not cry but I could of just started to
cry right then. What was I a dog begging for a bone and just because I
had an injury, I am a piece of dirt. That is how I felt. I got over my hurt
and went into another post office about thirty miles away from home and

talked with that Postmaster. The same thing happened. I can't believe it, damn it, I will never work for them again. All those years for nothing.

I talked with another woman that she receive a neck injury and had to have surgery and had a scare on her neck and that the postal service would not let her come back to work and that was because of that she had to collect all of her retirement fund. She now is in the retail business.

He then took an in-home course on accounting and then went out and immediately became a bookkeeper at a local furniture store. He was happy for the first time since all this had happened to him.

I remember a woman that was dispatching a container of mail and the top lid of the container fell on to the top of her head. She also lifted all kinds of heavy packages and would put them into the containers and then one day her left arm would start hurting and she continue to have a sever headache over and over. Then come to find out that one of her vertebra's spine her neck was injuried. She was taking so many muscle relaxants that she was unable to go to work. The post office would not give her work to do at the job site. She just needed to stay home until she was able to work. After a year or so she then got surgery and then she was able to use her left arm again and because of being out of work for so long, she too decided to retire from the post office and take her retirement money.

I knew of two men, well into the age of fifties and was working at the postal service for many years. They have been picked on and been made a fool of and treated like dirt. Both men have gotten so mad and upset that one of the men said he was coming in with a gun and blowing the head off of the supervisor. The post office gave that man a full retirement because he was so distraught. The other man they picked on and made his home life so bad because he was so upset all of the time thinking that he might get suspended for whatever reason and that made him in such a mess mentally that he told his son while he got his riffle and was leaving in his truck, do not worry, things will be better.

The family knew that something was wrong and they waited. What he was off to do with that riffle. Come to find out he was on his way to the post office where he worked and was going to kill his Postmaster or supervisor because he knew that they wanted him out of the postal service and if that was the case, he was not going out without a fight.

He did come into the post office with his riffle and told the Postmaster that he was going to kill him. They managed to talk with him and assured him that they would give him a full retirement and his days of worry were over. He did not kill anyone that day. He retired all right and was a happy man at home until about a year later he was told that he had cancer and about a year after that he passed away at home with his family.

CHAPTER EIGHT
SEX IN THE POSTAL SERVICE

Every couple of years this post office would hire new people. It usually was about twelve clerks that would work as optical carrier route sorters of the mail on these machines or just mail processing clerks that would work up front to help customers at the window with customer service. We also had clerks that would sort the main in the cases. Then they would hire letter carriers to sort and deliver your mail to your homes.

In every part of the post office, including office management to maintenance people there is sex going on. By no means, I mean to say that all the people in the post office is sleeping with each other but there is those in that particular field that are messing around. They will meet each other right after work or on their days off and have a sexual encounter. It might last a long time and it might not. I have seen both happen in my many years in the building watching all of this happen before my eyes.

One woman, which was a supervisor of the bottom workroom floor, which was also called, the dungeon floor. She was in charge of that floor; she was the supervisor of the mail handlers but could tell anyone on that floor to do what so wanted them to do.

She looked and come to find out she was a woman who was loose and just would have sex with any man that would let her at any time and any place. She was about in her mid forties and had badly bleached blonde hair and wore a lot of make up. Her face was worn and had many years of either alcohol or drug use, but she was smart enough to get a position work within the organization of the postal service. Her name was Linda.

One story about her that I was told about after coming back from my two days off was that Linda was doing it again, and this time she really got her kicks off with more then one man.

She scooped out this one mail handler on the floor and started to flirt and see if he was interested in her and if he wanted to get to know her a little better that night. Then she asked him to go up stairs with her and of course this was the gravy yard shift so there were almost no one working up on this floor where all of the office personnel would work during the day shift. The only person that would be up their sometime of the night would be the janitor and I am sure she knew or figured out when he would be done with that area of cleaning.

She would always were short skirts and low tops to revile her breasts, if you could not see them then she would wear very tight tops so you could see the size and outline of her breasts. She would get very close to all the men on the floor and if she could rub up against them on the floor. I am not sure if she was with any woman from work.

She then had this particular man follow her upstairs to that personnel office and went to one of the back offices and with the lights on low. She then started to kiss him and of course, he was willing and wanted to get some free sex that night, so he kissed her back. They kissed and kissed and then she started to take off all of her clothes and so then he did the same. Then she got on top of the desk and then he started to kiss and suck on her breast and she started to make noises. He then moved to her woman hood and started to play with her. She was making even louder noises. Well, little did they know that the janitor came back up onto that floor to finish mopping that floor and went by that room and heard the loud noises and then saw them? He was shocked; he did not know what to do.

He went down stairs and told one of his friends that worked on the mail handler's floor because he knew he could talk with him about what he saw. This mail handler said that he would take care of this situation and wait for awhile before going back up there.

Then this mail handler whose name was Fred told about four of his co-workers about what was going on upstairs. Then Tom, Mark, Frank and Tony went upstairs to that office and to check it out for themselves. They saw them just getting it on. They were engaged in intercourse at this time and both of them on top of the desk, they were going so hard and heavy that they did not even notice that four other guys where there watching them.

Of course, this made these four men Tom, Mark, Frank and Tony get excited and have a hard on so they walked into the office and confronted Linda and this guy. They both were stocked and he instantly got off of Linda and got his pants back up. She did not care at this point what they thought. I was told that she was more excited to know that more men were watching her. Someone said that she used speed all the time when she was at work.

They told me at this point she then smiled at each one of them and noticed that they had a bulge in their pants and said, "Who would like to be next?" Then Mark said, what the hell, and then he said I am next. She then said come on over here. He then took down his pants and tight underwear and then got right on her and they went at it. Once he was done, she said who is next? All of them had there turn with her that night. Of course, she told them do not say anything to anyone about this, ok.

It was the talk of the whole first floor for about two months thereafter it occurred. You would see Linda smiling at these men as they walked by. I do not know if this happened more then this one time, but I would not be surprised if it did happened at different places because she would go to the local bar after work. There was a bar that opened at 6 a.m. that all wanted to go to after working all night to get a drink before bedtime would go and relax before going home. They would also play pool.

She would go in there and who knows how many she then had before going home to rest. There were clerks that would work on the letter sorting machines that would work very close with each other because you would have to relieve that person that is sitting in that chair and then you would sit down and start keying the three digit number of the zip codes of each piece of mail that would come in front of you on this machine. There would be a letter come in front of you for each second and you must key in the numbers or a code number which was either a two digit number or three for each letter.

The supervisor would take a edit of each person throughout the day or night shift to make sure that the people sitting down on the machine was doing there job right. After each edit, the supervisor would then want to talk to you in regards to that edit and tell you that he or she would run another one and put your score on the edit sheet. If you where to get or miss three or more letters wrong per each edit then you would be watched carefully and if it continue then you would go in for more training or be suspended for a week or two and if this edit problem continued after all of this then you may be in jeopardy of losing your job.

This is why years ago your letters would go to the east coast, west coast and be late coming to you. It would go there and take about two to three days to get moving onto the correct direction of where it was to go in the first place.

I knew one lady that I worked around and was pretty good friends with, her name was Judy.

Judy was in her early thirties and had a daughter from her first husband, which ended in a really bad divorce. Her daughter was about five years old at this time when I started to work with her. Judy was very pretty, long brown hair and she was about 5' 11" and her face was naturally pretty. She did not need to wear any make up. Her breast size was about 36 C and a small waist and long beautiful looking legs.

Most of the men that went by her always gave Judy a second look, married or not married. She worked with me on the letter sorting machines and we were on that machine for about two years together.

We would talk about our home life and her daughter and about her love life. I, after a while of getting to know her would have her over to my home or go out with her to have a drink and talk. Then, about a year after I got to know her, I noticed that she kept looking at this man over on the next machine next to us. This mans name was Michael. Michael would look over and smile at her often. I then asked her when I was in the back of the machine with her, did you see Michael looking over and smiling at you? She said, yes I did. Then she said to me, he is the one that I have been having a love affair with. I said he is the one, yes he is the one.

I was shocked, Michael was a married man and had four boys and from what I heard is that he had a very beautiful wife. A wife that had long blonde hair and a little body and worked very hard taking care of him and their four boys.

Judy said to me, why don't you and I go out for a drink after work and I will tell you everything but you must promise me that you will not tell anyone about this. I love him so and I know that he loves me, too. I said sure, lets go do that after work. I never did tell anyone, I keep it all to myself.

We then went to a place called, Joe's and sat where we could talk without anyone hearing us and that no other postal people would be there. She then told me how they met at the post office and how he invited her out to lunch and they became good friends first. He said he needed someone to talk to about his wife.

She was so beautiful but so controlling and so busy all of the time and not having enough time for sex and being with him. You know what it is like to work these hours and then come home and try to get some sleep, he said. When you wake up, you then want some good time with your spouse and kids. Michael said he liked sex and wants more of it, but she is so busy she doesn't have time for me. I do not know what to do.

Judy said, that she understood and felt sorry for him. She was alone and had a bad divorce and had her daughter but was looking for the right man. She then told me that he was so handsome looking and she was in such a desire for a sexual relationship and it just started up like that. She said that the sex was the greatest that she had ever, ever had. He was so good in bed and that they would make love for at least three to five hours every time they were together.

I wondered why she would come to work very tired many times. She told me that she loved him so much and she hated to do this to his wife and his kids but she could not stop. I asked her, how does he hide it from his wife and kids? She said, that he told me that he lies and says that he has a postal activity that he must go to do and he must do it for his job.

I felt so sorry for her because there where so many good men out there that was single and would give her the world if only she would ask for it and be interested in them. I could see that he would never give up his wife and four boys to marry her and start a life with her because he would flirt with other woman at work when she was not looking. Any man that would have such a sexual relationship and still flirt with other woman is just using that woman just for sex.

I would tell Judy that she needed to go out with other men and look for a man that would love her and provide a life for her and her daughter, but she said that she has been thinking of that because she is not getting any younger and wanted to be married again some day. But, she said that she has been thinking of Michael and she just could not stop her relationship with him.

So I watched this love affair go on for about four years and I moved on into another post office and I have often thought about her and wondered what has happened with there relationship. I hope she found someone that would love her and her daughter and she would stop being used by Michael. I just prayed that God would send the right man into her life some day.

Another woman by the name of Julie was very distasteful in my point of view. She started right before my group of people came in. She would do things to get men's attention to look at her. She would where the tightest pair of pants and lots of make up and just walk around where the men could see her.

I remember that about two years after working together with her on the letter sorting machines, she would then start wearing the push up bra's, but this was not the regular push up bra's, these that she wore was the bra's that would push up what you had but would have a open hole where your breast would be exposed and would look just like you almost where not wearing a bra and your nipples would be exposed and you could see them easily when she got cold. She loved doing this. She also took speed everyday at least at work, I knew this because she offer me some but I would not take any because they did do random drug test and I did not want to lose my job.

There were many women and men that would go out to their cars in the parking lot and have sex or drink while they where on lunch and come back in afterwards.

Every year we all would hear of about twelve to fifteen marriages breaking up because one of them where having an affair with someone here at work. People like supervisors, head foreman to the clerks and mail handlers. The carriers we did not hear about because they worked days and we never worked or got to see them much because we always worked swing or grave yard. During Christmas time we would see them more because we would have to work ten to twelve hours shift of course.

By the time of the tenth or twelfth hour, all I wanted to do was to go home and go to bed.

CHAPTER NINE
STEVE'S CHILDHOOD

I was able to sit by and to talk with Steve many times in the long six months of training for our letter sorting machine positions. We had many decisions of many different things. I came to learn many things about everyone's lives and especially Steve's. We were one of the quite ones in the group. I like to talk as a woman usually does, but I did it when I could work and talk at the same time. Steve became like a close trusting friend to me. He knew that he could tell me anything and I knew the same about him. It was about a year after we were working together that he told me about his marriage and some of the problems at home he was having. I listened and tried to give my advice as much as I knew about marriage. My marriage was over, but I was married for eleven years and knew it was time for this relationship to be over.

I listen to every word that he had to say to me. He then began to tell me about his childhood. We were in the dungeon, as they called it, in this post office. He felt like no one else could hear because we were all alone and he knew he could trust me. I will never forget what he had to say to me regarding his childhood. We knew that we could talk without being interrupted because we were to be in this location for hours. This was the only work for us to do for most of the day. So we talked and throw letters into the case.

He began to tell me that he grew up in the mid west, Nebraska State. What his house looked like, because he lived there all his childhood before he was old enough to move out and get away from that area and from his father and mother. He said that he had four other brothers and two sisters all younger then he was. He said that he was the oldest and that he had more responsibilities then all the rest of the kids. He then asked about my childhood and if I had a good or bad growing up years.

I began to tell him of some of the abusive years that I went through growing up. I said, I was beaten by my alcoholic mother once because she could not find some keys in the living room and was asking me were did I put them? Then she came at me and just started to slap my face over and over again while I walked backwards to try to get away from her and as I stepped backwards she would step closer and slap my face again and again. He said, yes being abused is no fun, is it? I said, no. I never want to go through anything like that again. He then began to tell me about his years of abuse.

He started by saying my father hurt me. He hurt me when I was five years old. He said never to tell anyone. My first brother was born that year. Mom seemed to be so busy with him. My dad would have me go outside to the barn to help him with cores around the farm that we had. At first, I thought great lets go but then after the fourth time of having my dad bend me over and hurt me so bad, I did not want to go any longer. Then he began to force me. I wondered why was my father hurting me this way.

My mom would say, you go with your father and get all those chores done or else no dinner for you tonight.

I wanted to tell her but I could not, I just did not know what to say.

One day, she saw blood in my underwear and asked me what this was all about? I just looked at her and could not talk, I was hoping she would figure it out, but she did not. She said, next time you have diarrhea, I will get you some medicine for it, ok. I could not say a word.

I was speechless, I wanted all of it to come out but I could not say a word, I just looked at her.

Then when my brother was four years old and I was eight, he started on him, my brother would come out of the barn crying and crying. He would say to me, I hurt, I hurt. I told him to come over here and lets go up stairs and I would help him, I would put some medicine ointment on his butt to help heal it. I would stay away from dad as much as possible, I told my brother to listen to me a stay away from him.

Then my other brother was born. We put up with fathers abuse until my third brother was about five years old. He started on him. I said to myself, enough of this. Our mom needs to know. So, I said to mom, can I please have a minute of your time to talk with you today, she said sure son, let's go sit down in the front room. She was also pregnant with our sister at this time.

I sat down on the floor by her feet and said mom, I want to talk to you about what has been going on, please listen to me. This is going to be very hard for me to say, ok. She said, yes son, I will listen.

I told her then that dad has been hurting John and me for years now. He takes us to the barn and has us bend over and he puts himself into our butts and makes us bleed. I told her I want it to stop.

She said, what? No, this is not happening, Steve you are making this up. I am a shammed of you. I said, no mom, this is true, please believe me. Remember the blood you found in my underwear that day. She just said, Steve I do not believe you, your father would not do such a thing to his sons.

My mother would not believe me. I then became bitter towards her and lost respect for my mother and father. I became angry with myself. I then had "self-hate" and feelings of inferiority about everything, who I was and who was I to become. Maybe just like my dad? No way. Was it my fault? I lost the biggest part of my childhood and I wanted to protect my brothers but I could do nothing to stop it. I just went through my growing years feeling dirty and worthless and then I felt like it must have been my fault.

When I was fifteen years old, my dad tried it again. I hit him with my fist and I used all the force I could mustard up to hit him with. I hated him for what he wanted to do to me. I was to go without dinner and then up to my room for two days because of my hitting him. My mother never asked why I hit him and dad did not say a word why I did it either. They told me to just stay in my room.

When my first sister was born, my father loved her very much. He was good to her. Then when she was about seven years old, our mother needed to go to town to finally get her hair done, she was looking forward to this trip so her hair would look nice.

She was gone for about four hours. That afternoon, dad ask June to come into the barn and help him, she did. When he was all done, she came out crying and crying. She ran into the house and went right upstairs to her room. I hear her crying because I was upstairs to at the same time she ran into her room, I was doing my homework. I knocked on her door and asked June if I could come in, I opened the door and asked, are you all right? She said no. I did not know what to ask her next, then I heard mom come in the back door saying, I'm home.

Then mom came upstairs and she could hear June crying. June was still in her room. Mom wondered why she was crying. She then went into June's room and found that her pillow was all wet from her crying. What is all of this, you're crying so much. June said, I hurt! Mom said, where do your hurt? June said to mom down here in my private spot, then mom told me to go into my room while she looked at June. I could hear this because my room was right next door to June's room, I could hear everything.

Then mom could see that she was bleeding from her private spot. I could hear mom say, you have been ripped opened, what caused this June? June said, daddy did this to me. Mom screamed, then I ran out of my room and into June's room. Then mom screamed again, oh my God, it's true what you said Steve!

Steve, I am so sorry mom said. I know now that it is true. Please forgive me. I said, yes mother, I have forgiven you for not doing anything back then.

Mom then asked me if I would go get the healing cream from the bathroom and I did. She then put some onto my sister and said for me to get your brothers and stay up here with your sister tonight. Please put your sister to bed after she eats her dinner in her bed and to check on her. Mom said, she would have a discussion with our father tonight. I said, yes mother, I will do these things.

Mom made dinner for us; she brought it up stairs to our rooms for each of us. I helped my sister with eating her food, I felt so sorry for her. I hated my father more now then ever. I wanted him dead.

I could hear my father come through the kitchen door. I peaked down the stairs; mom was sitting at the kitchen table. Come sit down, George she said. I have something to say to you.

Why, how could you hurt our children so??? How could you have sex with your child like that?? You hurt our little girl for life now. I'm not good enough for you? You no good bastard, I hate you, mom said. If I every hear of this happening again, I will kill you.

Then I saw our dad come over and slap our mom's face. He said, don't you ever say that to me again? I will kill you and each of the children if you or they say anything, got that!

I could then hear our mother crying down stairs. Then later that night she came up stairs and looked into each bedroom and made sure we were all right.

When my father tried to get alone with me again, I hit him with my fist again. He tried to hit me but he missed and fell down. I told him, I hate you and I will kill you if you try it again.

He was able to get my other brothers a couple more times sexually but then I told them to fight him off and then they did that, too.

Steven asked me, why would a father do that to his children? I said, I do not know. I think that is the sickest thing a parent could do to their children. I would hate him too, I said.

Carolyn, he said to me, it has hurt my adult life. I do not feel I am good enough in bed for my wife. I feel like she could do so much better then me for a husband.

I get angry all of the time at the littlest things. I am not the most passionate man. I am sad and moody all of the time. I hate this job because I cannot be home with my wife at night. I miss my family. I tried to get into see a counselor and went twice but then the post office called and said to come in to start training. I do not know if I will ever get over what has happened in my childhood.

What do you think? I think you are a great man, what you went through was a trouble thing that no child should ever go through. It is not your fault. I think Steve that you have trouble inter-acting with others because of what has happened to you. You do need some help from a doctor to get over the pain. I needed help; I went to a doctor and went several times so I could come to understanding, why? Why me and how could a parent do those bad things to someone who is so little and helpless and trusting of a parent. How?

I got answers and you have not gotten answers, yet. I said, that it is apparent that you grew up in a dysfunctional home and your father is a sick man. Your father also abused your mother, if she did or said anything to anyone about this. You children were abused in the worst way. You have the right to be angry! You children were the innocent victims.

You have invariably bear the scars that have lasted for years now. If you do not work through the pain of this bad thing that you have experienced you and your family will suffer for the rest of your life. I came to a new understanding that Steve had failed to learn appropriate and effective behavioral responses to some or several frustrating situations in life. He seemed to have a moderate disorder. He was showing erratic behavior.

Your father was a sick man, possibly he got this sickness from his father or grandfather or someone in his family that did this to him.

It was not you, you did not ask to have this done to you, and you did not desire it. Your father also became a wife abuser; he took the truth out on your mother. I would also believe that he hit your mother more then you knew about. You just did not see it.

Steve, I read many books about abusive home lives, because I went through it, too. This is what I learned.

These things that have happened to you and your whole family has caused problems in your adult life could cause for example, chronic bed-wetting, violent behavior towards other children. When you reached adulthood, some problems like feelings of always being caught up in excessive anxiety and worry to violent, aggressive criminal activity. Your father when he was caught in his "sin" then turned his shock and anger back onto your mother.

And, you must of though as a teenage, "Now see what you've done, it is all your fault. You've kids caused your father to hit your mother. Your mother, for whatever reason, neglected you kids, you where honest with her and she did not believe you. This is your mother's fault. She was wrong and for the rest of her life she will have to live with this. You did the right thing.

Remember, many mothers who are regularly abused become so emotionally tied up with her own emotions that they neglect the care of their children, particularly young children. You see, studies show that the neglect is abandonment, lack of supervision, nutritional neglect, medical/dental neglect, inappropriate or insufficient clothing, hygiene neglect, and lack of proper shelter as well as educational neglect.

Steve, you know that I used to wonder what was wrong with me, why did my mother do these mean things to me? Then I read some books and also learn that, children that have been abuse and neglected suffer from things like: being constantly hungry, having unattended physical problems like untreated wounds or lack of dental care problems, having malnutrition and lack of supervision, and one of the most interesting for me is having poor hygiene like torn or dirty clothing.

Did you know that a sign of emotional maltreatment is: 1) speech disorders, 2) retarded physical development, 3) a failure to survive syndrome. You see you are no different, you have suffered and I have to a certain degree but you face the past each and every day and now the day to day life of working at the postal service, it is not easy to be in this situation.

The one family that I think about is Sheri, Tom, Cass and Alan, Don and Joy. This family, the brothers and sisters now sum up their grown up life; is that they grew up feeling a need to pretend in their adult life. Sheri said, that none of us finds worth in who they are. They all hide behind or within some sort of pretense out of a strong childhood need to be human. They all learned that who they are is not good enough, and we have no assurance that someone like our father won't come along and make us suffer because we aren't acceptable in his or her eyes.

Steve, I was an adult child of an alcoholic mother and never had a father figure around.

Steve you are a wonderful man. I can tell that you love your wife and your children. Your children love you and you work hard and I am so proud of you. I have been so blessed to meet you and be able to talk with you. I hope that I have been somewhat of help to you. I do know that what you have been through has not been easy on you but rest a sure that there is a God. His son, Jesus Christ paid the price for your father's sin and everyone's sin's on the cross. I have had to forgive my mother for the pain and suffering that she has caused me. It has by no means been easy to forgive her but it has been a matter of the heart. If Jesus could go through the pain and suffering for me, I can surely forgive my mother for the mistakes she has made. How about you?

Steve said, I guess your right. I can see myself with a lot of those problems. I have bitterness and I tell you the truth I do not know if I can get over it. I have this sadness and I just cannot shake it. I think I need help.

I told him, please get some help. It will only help with the marriage and your children as well as your outlook here at work.

I told Steve that I just take this work place as a place to come to work and to earn a wage and then go home. I do not let the people who are in charge get to me and I feel so sorry for them because they are not happy people inside.

Don't you think the same thing Steve? He said yes, they are the most sorry sites of people I have ever seen. I just want to be lifted alone. They will not leave me alone. Especially, the ass hole Forman, you know who I mean. Yes, I do. Steve said, I do not mind sitting down here in the basement where I know that they will be leaving me alone. I do know that I can not take that one supervisor that we worked under for what was it, six months where you could not say a word Carolyn to anyone and we just would work so hard and just no thank you for it.

Some days it feels like I can only take so much, Steve said.

CHAPTER TEN
THE GUN

The letter sorting machines where down for repair for a while so they sent the people from the machines everywhere else to do some other mail processing while they fixed and repaired the machine. I went over to the states mail processing case where not many people wanted to go because it was so boring to work there.

I came over to the cases and sat down next to Steve who I started to work with in the beginning of my postal service career. I said, hi Steve and started to work the mail into the slots of all the states, it is the miscellaneous mail that was not able to go through the machines and this is the last place where the pieces need to be done by hand and then it will go to that state and processed in that town's zip code.

I noticed that Steve seemed so depressed or worried so I knew that I could ask him anything because we have worked together now for at least two and a half years and have gone through many things her at this post office.

He then started to tell me that he is planning on bringing in a gun to kill the foreman that is on this shift. How he has worked him so hard and given him so much overtime that he is not able to spend time with his family. Steve said that he has asked this foreman if he could please not work anymore overtime because his family needs him at home, it's a personal matter and it is very important that I come home right after work.

Steve then told me because of working so much overtime; his wife is planning on leaving him and taking the children with her. I could see in his eyes that he feared that she is also thinking of getting a divorce.

He was just about in tears telling me all of this. I, for a moment, did not know what to say or do. I was a born again Christian and then began to pray to myself. God, please help me to counsel with him and help this situation. I did not want him to kill anyone, but I must say that this foreman was really bad to Steve and should have never treated any person the way that he has treated Steve.

I knew that this point that Steve wanted to inflict the punishment for the way he treated many people and for possible cause problems in Steve's marriage.

Steve then said, he was so rude and careless of people's lives or feelings. He did not care if you just had heartache. You better do the job and do it right now. He also wanted you Carolyn to sit a curtain way on the stool and you better not say a word to anyone. I said to Steve, he seemed to be a very unhappy man himself.

I began to counsel with Steve and tell him that I understood how he was feeling but I said to him that even if you killed this man, you would not be around for your wife and children. So killing him was not the answer. You need to tell your wife just how much you love her and the children and please do not leave me. You my wife are my world. I love you so much because do not leave me because of my job. Tell me what you would like me to do to fix this situation.

I told him that maybe you can look into transferring into another office where you can become a letter carrier or a mail handler. Do something so that you can get away from this man and save your future. I said, please, please do not do something that will harm you any more then what has already been done to you so far. Please listen to my advice and do this.

I will pray for you Steve, I will pray that your wife will see how much you love her and the kids and that things will change.

He said, yes. He said that I have to get away from this terrible, worthless, un-human man who is our foreman. I must do this so he does not continue to harass me everyday. I just cannot take it any longer.

I feel like I am going insane. I cannot sleep when I get home. I am always worried about my family and so I come home after work and my mind is running from the minute I laid down and keeps repeating over and over again that she is thinking of leaving me and the hurt from that and then how that ass hole foreman keeps treating me and belittling me every day at work and I do my work but he keeps treating me this way and I do not know why.

I have not missed any time at work because of my home life and I am always ready to work. You know that we must not miss any work so here I am to do the job.

So here I come into work everyday and as soon as I get here, here he comes and is all in my face. He tells me that I am not doing a good enough job, I am slow and I better speed up or else he will have me report to the blue room and put me on suspension if I do not improve my speed or give him any lip.

This foreman is a black man in his early fifties and is starting to get some white hair; he is about 5'7" and weighs about 145 lbs. He looks very old and rugged, he always talks loud and acts like he is a commander and chief of the President of the United States and you better listen to him or else. He was a very unpleasant man to be around. We did not have anything against him being black. Steve and I have had many friends that this post office who were black.

I felt that this man, and I mentioned it to Steve, that he was a very sad person inside and deep down, I thought, because he was always angry at everyone and everything that something in his life was making him this way.

He smokes and when we have seen him in the local bar, he drank many drinks while we were there and one of our members of our crew heard that he was into crack as well. I told Steve that I just knew that I did not care to be around him, I managed to keep away from him until he came up to me that one afternoon while I was working in the letter cases, I was sitting on one of the postal stools that they gave us to sit on and throwing the letter mail into the slots where they needed to go and as fast as possible because the mail must move and get to the truck docks so these letters could get on the next truck out of this post office and on its way.

He came up to me and said, I heard that you are the Bible lady that you have gone around talking to people here on the floor about Jesus and God. Is this true? I said, yes. I have talked to people about why I am smiling all of the time and I have shared my faith through conversation with other people here at work.

He then started screaming at me, do you remember that part, Steve. He said yes. I then said do you remember him saying, you better never do that here again, you Bible thumpers you. If I hear of you doing this again, I promise you that you will wish that you were never born. I do not want to hear of another word from you. How dare you go around saying that stuff? I will send you home and make sure you will have several weeks off and sit up right on that stool, put your foot on the bottom of that stool, if I catch you sitting without your foot on that bottom part of that stool I will call you into the blue room and speck to you even more, do you understand that, I want to hear you say, Yes. Also, I want to hear you say that you will never bring that name of Jesus up in this post office again, so you tell me now that you will not, I repeat, will not bring that name up here in this post office again.

Well, he said to me Steve. Well, I am waiting to hear you say that you will not say that name. I do not hear you. Do you understand what I am saying to you, Carolyn?

I told him, yes, I 'hear what you are saying'.

I would not tell him that I would never speck that name of Jesus in this post office ever again. It was my right to talk about my Lord and Savior if people wanted to hear about my life. I will always pass on what has changed me and how I feel so much better in life then I used to.

I though about it Steve, and I realized that this man has no love in him. His life must be living hell on earth. He has no feelings, no love, and no caring. His life must be all about getting work done here in this post office and so he can get his raises and move up to the next promotion.

Steve then began to speck again. He told me that he was so worried because he could not get fired from this job. I bring home good money and do not know what else I would do.

He seemed like he was ready to have a nervous breakdown right there. I told him that he is just a good man and how I respected him so. I said, you know that your wife sees how you have worked so hard; she just doesn't understand the abuse that you and other people here get from the upper management while working. It seems like they take pleasure in giving people like us, the beginning workers who have only worked about two years a whole lot of harassment. It is only when you have worked here in this post office over three years that you seem to get a break from the bad treatment and you become a human being just like they are.

The upper management usually is retired military people and that is why the postal service hires them so they can keep the new employees in line and make them work.

Keep them working for hours at a time and they better only be gone on their break for ten minutes. If any of them look like they are not meeting the standard working practices then keep at them, break them down until they have it in there heads what to do and you make them into a hard working machine. If you do not, you will not receive a raise in pay, got that.

I then thought, that is so true. I remember seeing them laughing at us in the local bar that we were in after a hard nights work. We came in and there they were. They looked at us and just started to laugh, remember that Carolyn. I said yes, I remember.

We know what they were doing, we just knew that we were better people then they were because we had a heart and cared at least for each other and did a good nights work and was not a kiss ass kind of person.

Steve then said that he just could not take it anymore. I should not do this but I just mentally cannot take it. I want my wife to stay with me. I told him, remember no matter what happens, your life is much more important and if you were to kill him, you would be in jail for many years and suicide is not the answer, because if you do that you will go to hell for killing this man and because God does not want people to take their life. God has promised everlasting life if you know Him and love Him with all your heart, mind, soul and strength. God will help you with this problem, just pray for help, and ask Him to help you. This is how I have gotten through everything here Steve. You remember what I have gone through, it has been no fun either and being told to go to the blue room and being abused here from him because I am a Christian.

God has gotten me through it all. I still feel blessed and happy no matter what the situation has been here. Steve then told me, you see him, that stupid son of a bitch, and that other general foreman where they think they can just rule your life. This is not the army and I refuse to be treated like this here. I just want the ass hole out. I want him dead. I have been thinking and planning on how I will use my 357-magnum gun on him. How I would walk up to him while he is lying on the floor bleeding and then ask if he feels like a bad ass, now? How does it feel to be treated like your life doesn't mean very much? You can die and no one will care about you here. How does it feel? Answer me now or I will shot again. I would love to hear him scream and the tone in his voice of being scared. I would shoot anyone who would come into my path to stop me, except you Carolyn.

I went out and bought the bullets yesterday. I am going home and polishing my gun tomorrow. I want to kill him; I can almost taste the sweet postal revenue on him. My post revenge upon that asshole. I bet that his family would be better off not having him because if he treats people here at work normally like this, how does he treat his family. They will be better off. He has caused us so much pain and suffering. I hate him, just as much as I hated my father.

I have been dreaming of this picture for months now. I first thought of poisoning him but that would not give the pleasure of everyone seeing him die. I want to see his blood all over the floor and see him in pain.

And, if he would ask why me? I would tell him, you have done such evil and you are evil, you do not deserve to live. It will be only the grace of God that you live.

Carolyn, I have also just though about shooting him over and over again until he is dead. I want to see the pain look in his eyes, just like the pain that he has caused me and so many of us on this floor. I just want no more pain.

I have seen him laugh at us and say how we are not hard working people and how he is going to whip us into shape. Well, that son of a bitch can just go to hell, where he belongs. I have had enough.

I then will turn the gun on myself, I will have two handguns ready and on me in cause I use up all the bullets on that ass hole from one of the guns. Then I will be able to just end it all for me. I do not want to go to jail. I know I will just become an old man in jail and become nothing. I do not want to live like that. I know my wife will marry again and I would never want to see my kids coming into a jail to visit me.

I will be helping any new clerks and all of you from any more pain and suffering from being treated like a dog, or better yet, treated like a prisoner in the concentration camps. We do not deserve it, we have done nothing wrong, we show up for work, we work hard by moving the mail and not talking and doing everything we are told to do. I cannot help getting tried by the work I do, I am not the fastest worker but I am here.

Remember Carolyn, the older guy who just had a heart attack at home last week, well he is now getting a "Letter of Warning" from our ass hole foreman because he has not called in and not able to come back into work because of his condition.

Now, that is just not right. Don't you think that is not right? Why would he do such a thing? I hope he will be in a lot of pain when he dies.

I then began to talk to Steve about wanting to kill the foreman. I told him, it just came to me that what I was just reading this morning before work. In the Bible in Proverbs 24: 8-12, it reads: He who plots to do evil will be called a schemer. The devising of foolishness is sin, and the scoffer is an abomination to men. If you faint in the day of adversity, your strength is small. Deliver those who are drawn toward death. And hold back those stumbling to the slaughter. If you say, "Surely we did not know this," Does not He who weighs the hearts consider it? He who keeps your soul, does He not know it? And will He not render to each man according to his deeds?

For a brief minute I thought about that and knew I was there for a reason. I needed to help Steve get through the pain and torment that this man had put him through. The hatred that I saw in Steve's eyes that night. I knew I needed to stay right by his side and talk with him. I ended up staying there for about four hours talking with him and listening to every word he had to say.

He talked in detail of the plan to kill him. I listened to him intensely, someone needed to take him seriously and believe me, and I did. I knew what it is to go through much pain that another person has caused you and knowing even as a child, you did nothing to get his type of emotional pain and suffering for. You were not the one that causes the circumstances that was in enforced but you were the one that person took it all out on.

I listened to every word now. I wanted to stop him anyway possible from creating a mistake in his life, one that he would never be able to change again. I also did not want to see this man killed, no matter how much pain he has caused, it was just not right to do so.

I wanted Steve to enjoy life and not let this man take the years away from him any more. I knew at this point, I was the one that God wanted to use and stop and care for Steve as well to listen to what he had to say. So go on Steve, I am listening. Tell me how you feel.

He talked and talked about that foreman and how he just cannot stand him. I have had it; I can't take it any more he keep saying over and over again. I have to do something about it. It must be done. He is no good, he deserves to die. He reminds me of my father. I wanted to kill my father and yet he still lives. I cannot stand by and let this man continue to hurt good people like yourself and the hard working people that work here. Don't you see, it must be done.

Steve, I said, have you talked with any other person about this. No, he said. You are the only one. You understand, don't you? I said, yes I understand your feelings and what this man has done to you and me in the last few months, but I am not going to let him hurt the rest of my days on this earth. I can see that he is in misery himself. He is going through some kind of painful life and he is just taking it out on you. He is like a time bomb himself. We are just in the way. Steve said, I couldn't take him any longer. I have had it. I have a headache everyday that I am here and afraid that he will come up to me and just start yelling at me. I am fearful each and everyday that I am here, I cannot wait for my days off, I have a break from this place then.

I asked Steve, have you talked with a doctor about this yet, remember last time we talked about going and seeing a doctor like I did to help me with my childhood days and help me get over the painful memories. I don't need to go to a doctor about this, I can handle it myself, Steve said. I said there is no shame in going and talking about this matter to a doctor. It is a real depression that you are feeling and you feel it each and everyday of your life if you do not get medical help, listen to me, please.

Steve do you remember what I said to you, I have gone to see a couple of doctors for my depression from what has happen in my childhood days. I have gone through so much, which I almost, as a young girl, just about had two nervous breakdowns before I reached eighteen years old. I needed to talk with someone that could help me with knowledge of: if I was the one to blame for what happened or if the other person who was giving the abuse was the one that was to blame. Do you see that is the healthy thing to do? You need to do this, I only say this to you because Steve, I care about you, this is not to say that I think are you crazy for that reason. It is for you to be able to cope with this man or anyone in your future that you may work with and to be happy with the rest of your life. You deserve to be happy and I want to see you laugh and smile. Will you please go do this?

I don't know, Steve said. Please go for me Steve. Steve you have held onto the pain from your childhood. You have not let it go, you need to let it go and get through the pain. You did nothing to deserve what you went through. Unfortunately, there are people in this world that are sick in the head. They take things out on children and you and I was one of them. I have dealt with the pain and suffering that I went through, I will never forget it but I will not let it continue to hurt the rest of my life and neither should you.

I am my own person now; I am healthy now in my mind. I am not the mirror image of my mother and father who hurt me so badly that I almost lost my mind.

This is what this foreman is doing to you, you are letting him bring up the pain and making you feel like you are nothing and you are getting close to a nervous breakdown now.

Do not let it happen to you. Stop right here and now. Go to a doctor. Call your health provider and see if you can get in on one of your days off and tell them you have an urgent need to talk about a situation at work.

And by the way, I work at the postal service. Believe me, they will get you in right away. I have talked with a doctor regarding the foreman myself and what I have gone through here and I feel no shame about it, I am glad I did it.

You need to teach yourself to break the worry habit and stop remembering what happened when you were a young boy. You need to deal with the pain. Whatever it takes to get it out. And don't be afraid to cry and get out the emotional built up pain that is inside you, this pain is for real and this is your feeling. This is the healthy thing to do. You can do it.

I want you to see the funny side of life. I would like to see you be busy with things with your family. Hear about your projects that you are doing. To see you smile a lot more of the time. You are a wonderful man. You must do your very best to help you. This foreman isn't going to help you. You are letting this foreman hurt you.

The way you stop him is to show him that you are more of a man then to let some angry person wipe your life out with words that he has no right to say to you or anyone for that matter. He is only venting out his anger out on us because of what he is going through himself. He himself needs to see a doctor, don't you see that. He is killing himself each and everyday and you want to kill him, you would take the right for him to become healthy before he dies. You must not kill this man.

Doesn't this all add up to you now? It is not you or I that caused his problem and only killing him would bring more problems to your world and your family would be crushed. They would be without you. I heard you that you wanted to kill him. You should not do this. It will not help, you will feel even worse then you do now. You will keep the cycle going on for yourself. Take the step of healing, please.

I then told Steve that I learned a very important fact about people that I looked at as my enemies. I told him that I read many self help books and I learned quite abet.

I said, when we hate our enemies, we are giving them power over us, power over our sleep, power over our appetites, our blood pressure, our health and our happiness. Our enemies would dance with joy if only they knew how they were worrying us, lacerating us, and getting even with us! Our hate is not hurting them at all, but our hate is turning our own days and nights into a hellish turmoil. Isn't that so, Steve?

Who do you suppose said this: "If selfish people try to take advantage of you, cross them off your list, but don't try to get even." I am not sure who said that but I believe it is so true. When you try to get even, you hurt yourself. How will trying to get even hurt you? In many ways, I read the personality characteristic of persons with hypertension, which is high blood pressure, is resentment, said by Life's Magazine.

See studies have been done to show how things like this can hurt you. I told him, when resentment is chronic, chronic hypertension and heart trouble follow.

So Steve, you see that when Jesus said, "Love your enemies," he was not only preaching sound ethics. He was also preaching twentieth-century medicine. When He said, "Forgive seventy times seven," Jesus was telling you and me how to keep from having high blood pressure, heart trouble, stomach ulcers, and many other ailments.

Steve, you see that foreman, remember what his face looks like, well consider this. His face has been wrinkled and hardened by hate and disfigured by resentment. All the cosmetic surgery in the world won't improve his looks half so much as would a heart full of forgiveness, tenderness, and love.

Hatred destroys our ability to enjoy even our food. The Bible puts it this way, "Better is a dinner or herbs where love is, than a stalled ox and hatred therewith in." Wouldn't your enemies rub there hands with glee if they knew that our hate for them was exhausting us, making as tired and nervous, ruining our looks, giving us heart trouble, and probably shortening our lives?

Even if we can't love our enemies, let's at least love ourselves. Let's love ourselves so much that we won't permit our enemies to control our happiness, our health and our looks. What I have told you, is from a book called, "How to Stop Worrying and Start Living," by Dale Carnegie. It made a lot of since to me. This is why I am happy in my life. Steve, you need to find yourself and be yourself, remember there is no one else on earth like you.

We must, for better or for worse, must play your own little instrument in the orchestra of life. You Steve must be what your experiences, your environment, and your heredity have made you. You are something new in this world. Be glad of it. Make the most of what nature gave to you. You can be proud of who you are. This is what I learned from going to a psychologist. I have had no shame in it. I promised myself that I would never, never become what my mother was, and take things out on other people.

You need to talk with a psychologist, get a clinical view of what you went through and see that you are not the one to talk in all this pain. You can be happy and not let people like this foreman ruin your life with his anger. I have not.

Please listen to me. The psychologist helps me to see that I was taking the power to turn a minus of experiences into a plus.

He said, yes I agree, you are right. He is getting to me this way. It is only hurting myself. I am not sleeping very well at home; I keep having nightmares about him. Thank you so much for taking the time to talk with me. I really appreciate you as a friend. I really do not want to kill myself and nor do I really want to kill another human being but I knew I couldn't keep going on like this. I see that you know what I mean by that statement.

I am so worried because I cannot get fired because I am so worried about work. I know that everything I do lately here at work is wrong. He keeps coming over to me each day and saying, "What is wrong with you?" Don't I know how to do this right? I fell like I just do not know what to do about anything any longer. I try my best to work hard and do the right job but with only a few hours of sleep because of working all this over time. I am only getting a few hours to sleep at home and I have been really wanting to make love to my wife but when I get home she is already asleep and I just can not wake her up I know that she works really hard taking care of our children.

I am beginning to feel like she does not want me and I am not a good enough husband for her and she might be changing her mind about our marriage. My head hurts all the time and I feel like I am getting confused about many things. Sometimes I think of suicide. I think my wife and kids would be better off without me sometimes. Then at least they would get the insurance money for my death from the post office.

You know Steve, you could become a letter carrier, remember I said this to you before. See you could get exercise by being a carrier and get some piece of mind by being on your own route and you would be out of here. You can do it. If you want. Remember you do have the time in service where you can do this transfer. Just go up to the personnel office and ask them about a transfer. I say these things to you because I care and do not want you to die or have you shoot anyone here.

I believe Steve that you and I have gone through the terrible types of things in life for a reason. God uses the weak in spirit people, people that have gone through the things that you and I have for a reason. Please listen to what I am telling you.

The Bible says that, God purposely chose what the world considers weak in order to shame the powerful. Your weaknesses are not an accident. God deliberately allowed them in your life for the purpose of demonstrating His power through you. He has done this for me. I felt like I was nothing for most of my life before I asked God to come into my life.

I prayed, Jesus, please forgive me for all my sins and come into my life because I need you. I am at my end. I am so depressed and do not know what to do any longer. And I am so happy today and feel so much different. God said in the Bible, that He has never been impressed with strength or self-sufficient people.

In fact, he is drawn to people who are weak and admit it. Jesus regarded this recognition of our need as a being "poor in spirit." It's the number one attitude he blesses. You see what I mean. He loves you as He did me. The Bible is filled with examples of how God loves to use imperfect, ordinary people to do extraordinary things in spite of their weaknesses. If God only used perfect people, nothing would ever get done, because none of us is flawless.

Now I feel encouraged knowing I am loved and He is helping me get through the bad things that has happened to me.

Steve, our weaknesses, or "thorn" as Paul called it in the Bible, is not a sin or a vice or a character defect you can change, such as overeating or impatience. A weakness is any limitation that you inherited or have no power to change. It may be a handicap, a chronic illness, low energy or a disability. You and I have emotional and trauma scar's. Many hurtful memories.

You need to do as I did. I choose to go to a doctor and admit my weaknesses about my childhood days. How and what happened to make me wanted to end the feelings of unworthiness, like I was nothing and not good enough for anyone, especially my bosses. Then once you have accepted the Lord, Jesus Christ into your life by praying and asking Him into your life. You will be weaknesses and then God can work to have someone help you to get over them, like I did.

Paul in the Bible said, for when I am weak, then I am strong. You must depend on God completely. You see, I am ministering you though my deepest pain that I went through.

I, too, may have been sexually abused, I am not sure. My mother has beaten me. I am strong and confident and happy now because of what God did for me. You see, my weaknesses made me to be more compassionate and considerate of the weaknesses of others.

My ministry on earth is to help people that have gone through the same types of pain.

You need to be honest with God, show your true feelings, not what you think you ought to feel or say. Confess some of the hidden anger and resentment at God for letting you go through what your father did to you. I am sure you feel cheated and disappointed with your life today but God can make everything that was bad that happened to you turn out to be good.

You Steve will then help someone just as I am helping you today. Don't let bitterness destroy you as the foreman has lived it each and everyday of his life while we have been here.

Having friendship with God. This is so important and this has changed me. By releasing my resentment and revealing my feelings is the first step to healing.

Steve if you act out and kill this man and yourself, no good will come of this. You may think it will but believe it will not. You and your family will suffer. Your wife and children will suffer the most here on earth.

Did you know Steve those unbelievers of the Lord think that Christians obey out of obligation or guilt or fear of punishment, but the opposite is true? I obey Jesus because I have been forgiven and set free, I obey out of love and have never been so happy in all my life. Not when I got married or had my two children. I feel reborn since I asked Jesus into my life. I have a new life now.

No one can put the past pain back onto me like they did when I was a little girl. This can be the same for you. All you have to do is to pray with me and accept that Jesus Christ died on the cross for you and you can ask for Him to forgive you of your sins. Ok then will you pray with me? After we pray, then you will have a "Purpose-Driven Life." You will be reborn as I have. You will then need to get a Bible and start reading it. It is God's word to you. He will show you many things when you read the Bible. He will be your new father now. He will show you real love in a way that you have never gotten. He gave that kind of love to me. I have never felt this type of love in all my life. Every other true Christian believer has felt the same way.

Please Steve, for your sake do this with me.

He said ok. Great, let's go into the back break room where not many people go into and we can sit in one of the corners of the back room so we can be by ourselves. No one will see us and be able to hear our prayer. I do not care if they call my name and want me to come back to the letter sorting machines, you don't worry about it either. I care more about you and will stay here as long as you need me.

If they do page me over the loud speaker, please do not let it interrupt you because it will not interrupt me.

We lifted the workroom floor and walked back to the second floor break room and thank God only one other person was in that room but he was in the front part so Steve and myself were very much alone.

I asked Steve to sit in the chair across from me. I told him; let me pray for you Steve. It might me a long prayer so just listen and there will come a time where I will ask you to repeat the words to God in our prayer. Are you ready, he said yes?

I started to pray and ask God please do not let anyone bother us while we are in this room. I ask God to change Steve's life through this prayer. To make him a new man. To give him strength. To give him a new beginning. And, most importantly to take away the pain from the past. Give him love from you God and let him feel re-born and a fresh new person with the love of a good father. Help heal the pain of his childhood. He said yes, Lord helps me.

I asked Steve, please repeat these words.

Lord Jesus, I come to you and ask you to forgive me of my sins that I have committed in my life and that you will make me a new person. Thank you for dying on the cross for me. Thank you for taking all the pain and suffering on the cross for me. Be my new father and let me feel your love for me. Take away all the hatred in my heart for these people and forgive me for holding on to it. I pray that you will change the mind of my wife and that she will see a new me and love me even deeper then she has ever.

I believe that God sent you for me and everyone else in this world to help and thank you for helping me.

In Jesus name. Amen.

Steve began to cry and cry, which I thought was good because that showed me that God was already starting to release the pain in his heart. I looked for tissues in the room and thankfully found some. No one came into the room while we were praying and that other man never came to look and see what we were doing.

After Steve finally stopped crying. He looked up and said, I do feel different. I feel great. I cannot quite explain whom I feel. I just said, I know. I told you that I felt the same and you will feel great for weeks and maybe months. God blesses you because you are a new baby in Christ. You are a new believer and God gives you this gift of love and except ness.

I told Steve, did you know that the Bible says that your name is now written in the book of life. That the moment you asked Jesus to come into your life, the angels in heaven had a celebration just in your behave. Then God wrote your name in on the book.

This is what it says in the Bible. Let me get my Bible from my purse and I will read it to you. Here it is, Luke 10: 20 …rejoice because your names are written in heaven. And another place that it talks about it is, in 2 Corinthians 5:17 says, Therefore, if anyone is in Christ, he is a new creation; old things have passed away; behold, all things have become new. Also, Romans 8:9 says, But you are not in the flesh but in the Spirit, if indeed the Spirit of God dwells in you. Now if anyone does not have the Spirit of Christ, he is not His. 10 And if Christ is in you, the body is dead because of sin, but the Spirit is life because of righteousness.

And Steve, most importantly these two scriptures, John 3: 16 "For God so loved the world that He gave His only begotten Son, that whoever believes in Him should not perish but have everlasting life. John 3:3 Jesus answered and said to him, "Most assuredly, I say to you unless one is born again, he cannot see the kingdom of God." That says it all Steve.

This scripture has just come to my mind that this is what Jesus wants you to know. John 17:9 "I pray for them. I do not pray for the world but for those whom You have given Me, for they are Yours. 10 "And all Mine are Yours, and Yours are Mine, and I am glorified in them. 11 "Now I am no longer in the world, but these are in the world, and I come to You. Holy Father, keep through Your name those whom You have given Me, that they may be one as We are. 12 "While I was with them in the world, I kept them in Your name. Those whom You gave Me I have kept, and none of them is lost except the son of perdition, that the Scripture might be fulfilled. 13 "But now I come to You, and these things I speck in the world, that they may have My joy fulfilled in themselves. 14 "I have given them Your word; and the world has hated them because they are not of the world, just as I am not of the world. 15 "I do not pray that You should take them out of the world, but that You should keep them from the evil one. 16 "They are not of the world, just as I am not of the world. 17 "Sanctify them by Your truth. Your word is truth. 18 "As You sent Me into the world, I also have sent them into the world. 19 "And for their sakes I sanctify Myself, that they also may be sanctified by the truth. 20 "I do not pray for these alone, but also for those who will believe in Me through their word; 21 "that they all may be one, as You, Father, are in Me, and I in You; that they also may be one in Us, that the world may believe that You sent Me. 22 "And the glory which You gave Me I have given them, that they may be one just as We are one: 23 "I in them, and You in Me; that they may be made perfect in one, and that the world may know that You have sent Me, and have loved them as You have loved Me.

The last verse is especially for you Steve. John 17:26 "And I have declared to them Your name, and will declare it, that the love with which You loved Me may be in them, and I in them."

I told Steve that Jesus really does love him and can you feel it? He said yes, I really can. It is amazing.

I asked him please do not kill this man or yourself. He said, I don't think I need to kill him any longer. I said, that is wonderful. Remember get that Bible and start to read it.

I asked Steve for a favor, you would please give me your home telephone number. I can call your wife and ask her to please not leave you and that you probably will be a better man now from our talk today here at work. That Steve will probably be a more loving and smiling person when he comes home. Please do not think of leaving until you talk with Steve and see that he may be different. I know that sometimes a woman will listen to another woman. It is like listen to the Oprah's show. People listen and learn how people feel and how change can occur in a person life. You do not have to go through the same pain. You chose to not go on with the abuse.

He said, ok I believe she will talk with you. I know that she has been lonely for another woman's friendship. I said, I would love to become her friend and stay your friend.

I will check back with you tomorrow or the next day and see how things are going. I believe I have tomorrow off and if that is so I will find you on the workroom floor and see how you are doing. Did you know that now, you are my brother in Christ and I am your sister in Christ. We are a family. Cool, right.

He went back to the states mail processing case and I went back to the letter sorting machines and told them that I had a little emergency and I could not get to a phone or to the superintendents room to let anyone know. I was so sorry but it was very important I take care of this emergency. Thanks and I went back to work. No one said anything to me, thank God.

I knew that Steve was so close to doing what he said he wanted to do. I knew he felt that his world was at end and this foreman should thank God that he is still alive today because he came very close to dying from a bullet.

I saw Steve the day after and he was still smiling brightly. He did look differently and I was so happy. He really was a new man. He told me that his wife said what has happened to you. He told her what he did with me by praying and asking Jesus to come into my life. She was also thinking about going to church and now they are looking together for a church to go to.

I told him that tomorrow I was going to call her and talk to her about things and just listen to hear and help in anyway I can.

You know Steve, things will be great now. Things still may come up that you have to work on but just do your best in life, always read your Bible and pray. One of the most important things to do is to pray. God bless you, I will talk with you later, and they are calling me back to the machines. Bye.

CHAPTER ELEVEN
THE SOLUTION

There must be a solution. I believe that we need not put just the retired or military Men out of the service in charge as a Forman and the top ranks of the postal service.

One of the main reasons there is deaths in the post office is because these people push so hard on these people that they fold and cannot take the stress that these People put onto them.

My people that I worked with were very up tight and emotional stressed out to began with. Mostly, because of having to take care of there families at home and making sure everything was ok because they knew that they would be at work for eight to twelve hours. They knew that they would not be able to come home in less an emergency.

Promoting Forman's should be on their people skills and how they communicate. Not how they can get people to do there jobs and as fast as they can do it. We need people with good emotional backgrounds. People that care and want to do there best and have a personal way of talking and showing disciplinary actions.

For example that should never take place. A man about the age of Fifty-one had a heartache and he went by ambulance to the hospital and was in they're for a week. When he came home from the hospital he found a letter from the post office given him a "Letter of Warning". The letter says that if you are late or sick one more time you will be suspended from the post office and having two or more of these letters you will be terminated.

So you see, even being with a heart attach which this man never asked for nor plan on having him my cost him his career in the post office. And also, this man had eighteen years in the postal service. Now this is wrong. This needs to stop.

Some people do wrong with their sick days off, because of wanting to go parties or what ever they wanted to do that night. I can see if they have a history of this type of parting and showing up late with documentation that shows they have not been home when they should of, when the post office has called to verify that they were sick at home. Then by all means, give them a letter.

But when a person has documentation of being in the hospital or sick with something and has a doctor's slip, no one should get a letter.

And all my years in the post office I never did hear of someone told they must take another drug test. You know, the on the spot drug test. My post office for a while had a nurse's room and a nurse on duty. Why did they not do drig tests?

I have no idea.

Ninety percent of the people inside the post office work very hard. The other ten percent they need to keep a watch on. But do they, no they let them get by with so many things. I know of two men that would get so stoned every night while working in the post office and that they could barely do there jobs. They would get stoned inside the post office and outside in their cars.

Another solution is to do a drug test of the supervisors and management. This should take place as well as testing other employee on the clock as well.

There should be schedule classes for management to take. They should do a personally test, a behavioral test and a communicational test that shows what there skill are in handling the employees.

For an example, one supervisor that later became a general Forman. This man was a supervisor at this time and he supervised a letter-storing machine. He was so anger each and every night. When he would talk to you he would scream at you. Most people tried to stay away from him and just do there job.

But when you needed to tell him information or ask what to do next, it became unbearable. This man needed some time out.

Management knowing that this man was going through a divorce and really had a hard time going through all the emotions of dealing with it, should have taken him off of this job and put him into a different position while he finished going through all the emotions and heart break circumstances that he needed to deal with. Not leave him there so he could take it out on us each and every day.

This is a story about Mike. He was an anger person that we had to deal with at work. At some time in his life he suffered some form of injury to his dependence or individuality and did not know how to help himself recover from it. He grew up believing that he was not an acceptable person. He was never affirmed for who he was. Now he is locked in a position of pain that produces an unending fountain of anger that continually needs to be vented. Many criminals are angry males from dysfunctional homes. Mike happens to have all the signs of a dysfunctional person. Mike blames his temper tantrums on the humans that he has to be around all of the time at work. How can he expect not to be angry?

It is a hellish world even inside the post office. So he brings his own hell home and spreads it around, then complains because home is not a happy place to be. We're all going to hell anyway, he told me one day.

He goes around spoiling for a fight with anyone that would fight verbally with him and then someone to blame for the fight. He has no real friends except other people just like him who complain and criticize everything and everybody.

What kind of friends are those? He repels good people. Even the people at his church seem to avoid him. They all tried to get close to him at first, but they soon gave up when he never responded.

His wife came to the post office just to talk with him at lunchtime. She may never leave this man who batters her and her children

Every time he has a bad day. And he always seems to have bad days.

She left the post office determined to try harder to agree with him, dead set to reaffirm him; after all, it isn't his fault he had a bad childhood.

Another person that had problems that I worked with was, Tom.

Tom was so macho when he was working. The first time I saw him I thought, now there's a real man!

When he walked into the room, everybody watched him. He looked confident and strong. Every woman was after him, married or not.

Fortunately, I got to know him better as a friend. He tried to make all the decisions of what kind of work we were going to do. I thought to myself, what is he doing, I am not married to this man. If I wanted to go work in a different area that is what I will do. I told him as soon as I could talk with him while we work. I had a problem. He said, what is it? I said, it is you. You are making decisions for me and not asking me what I want to do. Stop it. He said that he was sorry. He does this all the time to his wife. He does not know why he does these things.

He told me what his wife said, she called me a drill sergeant that she had to live with. That I have to have my way. Nobody else has anything to say. Tom started to talk about his high school days, he called it his glory days. I think that maybe he is stuck into the high school days where he thinks he can get away with anything he wants to do.

I think men like Tom look and act very powerful. They are obsessed with their appearance and how they look to other people. I found out that he specks four different languages. And when he is at home he works out a couple of hours before coming to work.

The power-thrusting male usually attracts other men as well as women, especially men who are not powerful and who have a need to identify with powerful people. Women who find these men desirable are those who, like and enjoy a strong "pillar" to lean on.

At first glance, the power-thrusting male looks like a dashing daredevil. The power-thrusting male does not just "play"; he has to conquer, to win big. If he loses, as soon as he finishes sulking he demands a rematch and will desire to win.

At work, he does everything for praise, and he expects it. He has to get all the promotions. He treats those who work under him like temporary people or servants. At home, everyone has to do things his way. He has no longtime friends; people get tired of catering to his need for power.

Did you know, although this type of male looks and acts powerful, actually?

He is just the opposite. People who have studied the power-thrusting male have several contradictory thoughts on the kind of person he really is.

One thought is that he is basically insecure and needs to display power to reassure himself of his masculinity. If you could open up his head you might find him riddled with insecurities. He covers them over with power thrusts.

Another thought is that he is "empty." He is unable to have deep feelings because there is no depth. All he is concerned about is the acquisition and display of male beauty and power. Everything he does orbits around this concern. This condition, generally speaking, comes from the need to overcome the feeling of being a nothing. He continually needs to be reassured of his position, power, and status. He sees that everything he is involved in puts a positive light on him, like a trophy case filled with people, light on him, like a trophy case filled with people, objects, and experiences arranged neatly so that he looks his best.

I have read that it might be another theory; it suggests that this male is so full of himself he cannot see anything or anybody else beyond himself.

Everywhere he looks he sees his own reflection – elevated and inflated. The world is his banquet table, and everything on it is for his personal choice and consumption. Every person around the table is there to serve him and cater to his every desire and fancy just as, in all likelihood, his indulging mother did.

He craves excitement; generally, he is easily bored and has to be entertained he needs to be challenged and is very dependent despite of his independent and rugged appearance. Since his image is more important then anything else, he expends little effort toward developing subtle inner qualities.

Relating to such a man is very tiresome, especially for his wife. Their relationship started off with a bang and then peters out after the initial excitement wears off. This means that his wife has to support the marriage from then on. I could see that his wife did this, too. He never talked much about her, just himself. He keeps saying, my wife says that she always has to be the mother and the father in our house. I don't understand her.

I did not say anything; I was just listening and thinking of what I read.

The power-thrusting male may, from time to time, come up with earnest displays of affection or devotion or love, causing his long-suffering wife to hang in there just a little longer, thinking that he may be starting to mature and settle down. But these actions are just displays with little internal substance.

Because he is concerned exclusively with himself, the marriage relationship never goes beyond the opening bang for him. Before his marriage can mature to the level of commitment, promise, and integrity, the power-thrusting male stops working at it and his wife has to provide their marriage with those qualities all by herself. After a while she gets weary of carrying the whole load and generally burns out. "There's no more left in the well. I've just dried up because there's nothing coming in to replenish the supply of love for him.

This is material that I read from having to go to marriage counseling myself. The book is called, "Dangerous Marriage," Breaking the Cycle Of Domestic Violence, by: S.R. McDill & Linda McDill.

I too, was in a relationship where this type of behavioral pattern was taking place. When I talked with Tom, I could just see his life style.

I felt so sorry for his wife. I could see that he could be violent, but I never asked about it.

I thought to myself, as a power –thrusting male, Tom's primary concern is the acquisition, display, and wielding of power. He is one of those men who got stuck in adolescence and was never able to turn competitiveness and the power drive, which are typical of adolescence, into sharing, caring, and nurturing.

This next bit of information is very important, especiality for woman. I want you to read the "Characteristics of a Potential Abuser." I hope this will help you to see the facts about any man or woman.

How can one recognize a potential abuser? People do not concentrate on possible problems in someone they hope to marry; or have a relationship with, rather a woman looks for all the good things that will make her home a happily-ever-after place to be. However, there are certain characteristics that manifest themselves during the dating process that will give a woman some indication of the kind of person her man will be after the knot is tied.

Characteristics of the dysfunctional male-are not always easy to spot. Such a man at first may seem very safe, secure, and dashing. He can have a sweetness and seductiveness that say, "I love you dearly, tenderly, carefully, softly, and gently." However, the presentation ultimately gives way to an impatience, forcefulness, and control that says, "Don't' cross me!"

I have personally seen this in one man in my personal life that I thought he was such a wonderful guy, boy was I wrong. Please read on.

One of the most notable of these characteristics is how he handles his anger.

If little things seem to set him off, do not make excuses for him: "Well, he's tired...

He had too much to drink. . He didn't feel well . . .I pushed him too hard . . .

No one is perfect." Rather, consider that he has never learned to handle his anger in a mature way. Another characteristic of a potential abuser is his inflexible and compulsive need to have things his own way. He may show this need openly, covered with prickly irritability, or he may candy-coat it in subtle manipulation so that you do not recognize it until one day you realize you never get your way. You always do things the way he wants you to.

Unfortunately, the average woman will not discover this autocratic, dictatorial man until she actually attempts to build a life with him. Then she finds that he is inflexible and intolerant. By then it is too late to do anything about it except get a divorce or seek counseling.

The primary question every woman should ask during courtship is, "How does he handle frustration and lavation?" If she sees flexibility, tolerance, and Level headedness, there is a good chance the two of them will develop a flexible, power-balanced relationship. If, however, he handles frustration, disappointment, and aggravation by getting pushy and overtly – or covertly – angry, the marriage probably will not be safe and secure for his wife and children.

Pushiness, grouchiness, intolerance, and inflexibility are indications that your man is a micro Napoleon; he needs free license, free rein, and total independence in his relationships-the qualities young boys seek in establishing their superior male mind-set as they are growing up. But by the time these boys reach manhood they should have developed more mature behaviors.

The next groups of abusers we will look at-the Underdogs-are those men who manipulate from weakness rather than strength. These men are also emotionally abusive, which is harder to pin down and escape from.

Next let me talk about the Alcoholic Male. The signs of being an abuser.

The alcoholic male abuser is classified as an underdog rather than a top dog because he is chronically afraid and in pain. Over a period of time, his avoidance of these issues builds up pressure; once a certain amount of pressure has been held in check and forced down below the threshold of his awareness, the alcoholic needs to ease the constant nagging pain and avoid even a twinge of it. He discovers that alcohol is a psychic anesthetic/analgesic at first, then a disinhibitor and releaser of pressure. When he drinks, the pain is numbed for a while, but eventually it swells and spills out in ugly forms. In short, he feels much better at first, and then he blows.

His family and those close to the spilling out of anger all suffer. However, the power he releases is more of a pseudopower, a reactive anger-strength, very unlike true strength is powerful and heady stuff to the alcoholic. He really gets caught up in it and its display. It feels good to blow off steam and, quite possibly, "blow away" those people he misidentifies as his Problem.

Steve in my story has been severely abused as a child. I think that is why he has had a hard time in his career in the post office. Because of his abuse from his father, he has never gotten help and it spread over into his adult life. He now is releasing all his emotions and the post office stress is getting to him.

The postal service needs to get organized better. They should put people like the gentleman that I just mentioned into an office job. Keep his mind on paper issues and not deal with people and stressful position each day.

Those that are doing drugs should be given a drug test. Even if they are a ten-point veteran. The veterans should get an easy type of job. They can take there time in the letter storing cases and put the mail into them and call it a day.

The postal service should not ride someone like in the army. I have seen it. It is like a drill sergeant telling you, you must do this, and get it done right now. Hurry it up boy, I said hurry it up. Get to it now. Did you hear me?

No, no person outside of the military should be treated like that. Everyone should get respect and try there best to do a good job. We never once were told that we did a good job.

The only time, I was ever told and I believe this goes true for everyone else in my crew. That the training to place the test would say to us. Very good, you did a wonderful job you will have no problems on the machines. You did it.

Congratulations, welcome aboard. That was all. And we all were very scared when we took those tests. To this day, I really liked that man that said you did a great job.